NAPOLEONIC

WARS

THE ESSENTIAL BIBLIOGRAPHY SERIES

Essential Bibliography
Series Editor
Michael F. Pavkovic, Ph.D.
U.S. Naval War College

For general and expert readers alike, volumes in the Essential Bibliographies series combine an authoritative historiographical essay and current bibliography on significant subjects drawn from world military history, ancient times through the present.

PREVIOUSLY PUBLISHED TITLES IN THIS SERIES

The Korean War
by Alan R. Millett

Roman Warfare, 300 B.C. to A.D. 450
by Michael F. Pavkovic

War in European History, 1494–1660
by Jeremy Black

War in European History, 1660–1792
by Jeremy Black

NAPOLEONIC

WARS

THE ESSENTIAL
BIBLIOGRAPHY SERIES

FREDERICK C. SCHNEID

Potomac Books
Washington, D.C.

Library of Congress Cataloging-in-Publication Data
Schneid, Frederick C.
   Napoleonic Wars / Frederick C. Schneid. — 1st ed.
     p. cm. — (The essential bibliography series)
   Includes bibliographical references.
   ISBN 978-1-59797-209-3 (pbk. : alk. paper)
   ISBN 978-1-59797-578-0 (electronic)
   1. Napoleonic Wars, 1800–1815—Bibliography. 2. France—History,
Military—1789–1815—Bibliography. 3. Europe—History—1789–1815—
Bibliography. I. Title.
   Z6207.N2S36 2012
   (DC227)
   016.9402'7—dc23

                                                                              2012014701

Printed in the United States of America on acid-free paper that meets the American National Standards Institute Z39-48 Standard.

Potomac Books
22841 Quicksilver Drive
Dulles, Virginia 20166

First Edition

10 9 8 7 6 5 4 3 2 1

For Sarah

CONTENTS

I have been fortunate to count some of the historians whose works are mentioned in this book as friends. The community of Napoleonic military historians is rather small and as a whole has a zeal for the study of this era. This enthusiasm is a product of our affinity for history, the adventure and its lessons. The study of Napoleon has produced an enormous body of literature ranging from the hagiographic to the vehemently anti-Napoleonic. The age of Napoleon was an era of revolutions in which romantic passions merged with enlightened principles. The wars of Napoleon and their subsequent interpretation are in many cases polarized. The eminent historian Georges Lefebvre understood the draw of Napoleonic history. He concluded his classic two-volume history of Napoleon with this insight:

> Here lay the secret of the fascination that he will exercise for ever more on the individual person. For men will always be haunted by romantic dreams of power,

even only in the passing fires and disturbances of youth; and there will thus never be wanting those who will come . . . to stand in ecstasy before the tomb.[1]

Lefebvre, a Marxist historian, held the chair of the French Revolution at the Sorbonne and had a clear vision of where Napoleon fit into the dialectic, but his impeccable scholarship reduced any appearance of overt a priori perspectives. He was an exception, and there are many bad, uncritical, and visceral histories that have been published over the years. They litter all camps of Napoleonic historiography and must be met with great suspicion. It is not the responsibility of historians to justify the actions and events, but to explain and understand them.

It is not the purpose of this book to explore Napoleon the man but to focus specifically on the military history of the Napoleonic Wars. Just as Steven Englund clearly defined his biography, *Napoleon: A Political Life* (2004), this book is concerned solely with the military history of the Napoleonic Wars. Each chapter, if taken individually and comprehensively, could be expanded to fill the entire book, but the purpose of this volume is to present the reader with a lucid understanding of the current state of English-language historiography. To that end, I have not addressed many of the nineteenth-century histories, unless they remain the standard work. I have also avoided extensive discussions of memoirs and diaries, unless part of the historiography. There is much more than what is presented in these pages. Those interested are advised to seek Donald Horward,

1   Georges Lefebvre, *Napoleon: From 18 Brumaire to Waterloo*, 2 vols. (New York: Columbia University Press, 1969), 2:370.

ed., *Napoleonic Military History: A Bibliography* (1986) and the monumental two-volume, Ronald J. Caldwell, ed., *The Era of Napoleon: A Bibliography of the History of Western Civilization, 1799–1815* (1991). They contain a definitive list of primary and nineteenth-century sources.

Historiography is a moving target. The bibliographies above were invaluable upon publication, but shortly thereafter they became outdated in prescribing the newest literature and interpretations. This book hopes to fill the twenty-year gap between their publication and the new direction of Napoleonic military history. Further, the nature of this series limits the discussion to English-language sources. There is much more if one is able and willing to read other languages. French, German, Italian, and Spanish histories of this era increase the offerings exponentially, possess a historiography that addresses their respective national histories, and are equally connected to the international dialogue of Napoleonic historiography. In short, however, the reader is encouraged to "start here."

I would like to thank Mike Pavkovic, a longtime friend, for asking me to write this book for his series. I particularly appreciate Michael Leggiere's friendship and willingness to take time from his herculean writing efforts to provide comment on many of these chapters. Nate Jarrett, my research assistant, helped assemble a bibliography of Napoleonic military history, which was invaluable. Lastly, my family's patience and moral support was critical to the completion of this work.

INTRODUCTION

The Napoleonic Wars is one of the most widely explored and popular subjects in the realm of military history. The exploits and exploitations of the French emperor have, for generations, lent themselves to worshipers and detractors. The historiography of the period is expansive, particularly relating to the campaigns personally directed by Napoleon. In the nineteenth century, the emperor began his own narrative of events through his recollections on St. Helena. This purposeful creation of a Napoleonic legend served to immortalize one of the greatest egoists since Julius Caesar.

The advent of the Second French Empire in 1851 under Napoleon III served to propagate the Bonapartist agenda, and many of the now classic and standard sources such as the indispensable thirty-two volume *Correspondence de Napoleon Ier* (1858–1869) were collected and edited by order of Napoleon III. Any Napoleonic historian who conducts research at the Château de Vincennes, *Service historique de l'armée du terre*, knows that the ease of researching this era is a product of the enormous work of the Historical Section of the French Army under the Second Empire. Although historians have benefited tremendously from these sources, the purpose of these works was clear—to disseminate the Napoleonic legend. Indeed, the *Correspondence* are not comprehensive but selective, and for more than a century similar volumes labeled *Correspondence militaire*, or *Unpublished Correspondence*, have appeared, with attention to those documents that did not make it into the "official" volumes. Most recently, the Fondation Napoléon in Paris produced several volumes of heretofore-unseen correspondence drawn from the archives. All of these sources are indispensable to the scholar but provide an incomplete picture of the period. The *Correspondence* includes only those dispatches sent by Napoleon. For responses, one must refer to collections of memoirs and correspondence of the marshals, generals, and monarchs of Europe.

The publication of these primary sources in France did not end with the collapse of the Second Empire, but in fact, the Historical Section of the French Army under the Third Republic exceeded the activity of its predecessors. The "humiliation" of defeat in the Franco-Prussian War 1870–1871 and the subsequent arms race and tensions with Germany at the turn of the twentieth century encouraged greater examination of the Napoleonic Wars. Histories of this period were not limited to collections of memoirs and correspondence, but the prolific nature of French historians produced "official histories" of the wars, including the monumental Paul Claude Alombert and J. Colin, *La Campagne de 1805 en Allemagne*, 5 vols. (1902). All of these primary sources provided fertile ground to grow the Napoleonic legend, establishing a predominantly

French perspective as the starting point for any research on this era. The result was a century of Napoleon's domination of the military history during his reign. This is not to say that the rest of Europe did not produce their own narratives—they did, but the quantity and popularity of the historical literature was only rivaled in Britain, where Wellington's victories during the Peninsular War and at Waterloo remained the anchor of British military history.

The Austrians, Napoleon's most persistent enemy after Great Britain, produced a minimal number of historical works on this period. Articles appeared during the nineteenth century in the specialist and official journals, *Österreichische Militarische Zeitschrift* and the *Mitteilungen des K. K. Kriegsarchiv*, but the official histories were limited to the series *Kriege unter der Regierung des Kaisers Franz* and appeared for the centennial of the Napoleonic Wars. The only two volumes of this series on Austria's role in the French Revolutionary Wars were published in 1905. For the Napoleonic Wars the series included *Krieg 1809*, 4 vols. (1907–1910). Furthermore, the Austrians published a detailed account of the wars of 1813–1815. Fifteen volumes in two sets were printed between 1911 and 1914: *Österreich in den Befreiungskrieg*, 10 vols.; and the incomplete *Befreiungskrieg 1813 und 1814*, 5 vols., ending only with the battle of Leipzig in 1813. No official history exists for the war in 1805. It is clear from the date of publication that the army's historical section was more interested in Austria's successes than in examining its abject defeat in 1805. All these histories appeared in the early twentieth century, as Prussian and German nationalist historians during the nineteenth century dominated the histories of the War of German Liberation.

There was a significant amount of historical literature devoted to Prussia's war against Napoleon, with a particular interest in the period beginning in 1813. The "War of German Liberation" worked well in the imagination of nineteenth-century nationalists, and specifically the myth that Prussia led this crusade against France. The histories of the *Befreiungskrieg* (War of Liberation) are quite exhaustive, and the German general staff published a few specialized and antiseptic studies of the Napoleonic Wars, but as far as the voluminous and popular nature of these histories, they paled in comparison to that which emerged in France.

Russian accounts of the Napoleonic Wars were completely unavailable to the wider European audience considering the language barrier. Russian histories written in French allowed certain access, but there remained an enormous lacuna in the historical literature. Eugene Tarlé's popular history of the invasion of Russia, based on Russian archival documents, only appeared in English in 1942 at the time of the Second World War. Russian military journals, such as *Voenno-Istoricheskii Sbornik*, did provide interesting studies, but again the availability of such sources to a larger audience was limited.

In fact, for the English-reading world the history of the Napoleonic Wars was drawn largely from Britain and France. F. Loraine Petre's dense military histories of Napoleon's campaigns remained the standard works on the subject. It is only in the past two decades that his works are being superseded as scholars breach the language barrier to access the sources in Germany, Austria, and Russia, permitting a comprehensive reexamination of the Napoleonic Wars.

The long-standing classic primary sources of the Napoleonic Wars remain Carl von Clausewitz and Antoine-Henri, Baron de

Jomini. Both experienced the French Revolutionary and Napoleonic Wars firsthand. Clausewitz served as a young ensign in the Prussian army in 1792, as a lieutenant colonel in 1806 at Auerstadt, transferred to Russian service in 1812, only to return to the Prussian army during the Waterloo Campaign. Jomini began his military career as an officer in the French army. In 1813 he defected to the Russians and spent the next two years in service against Napoleon. Jomini initially had the most profound impact on the understanding of the military history of the Napoleonic Wars and Napoleon's art of war. He became a highly sought military adviser after 1815; his book, *The Art of War*, is entirely technical in its approach. Most European military institutions read Jomini, and his impact on the shaping of military systems and tactics in the nineteenth century was significant.

Carl von Clausewitz is often seen in hindsight as the more profound of the two. This notion is entirely a product of twentieth-century perceptions. Clausewitz's philosophical approach, *On War*, was published posthumously, and it was a reflection on the changing nature of war from Frederick the Great to Napoleon. From the twentieth century to the present, Clausewitz's discussion of the intersection between the military and civilian worlds is well known: "War is a continuation of policy by other means." Nonetheless, it was Jomini who dominated much of nineteenth-century military thought through the Wars of German Unification. Napoleon III turned to Jomini in 1859 to provide advice on a plan of campaign against the Austrians in Italy. Indeed, Jomini's book was discussed extensively at West Point, long before Clausewitz was available in English translation. It is Clausewitz, however, that provided several solid analytical campaign histories, of which only a few have made their way to English. Clausewitz's history of the Russian campaign in 1812 is extremely valuable, as is his history of the Waterloo Campaign. His books on the campaigns of 1796, 1799, and 1813 are equally important but have not been translated.

This book examines the changing nature of Napoleonic historiography in the English-speaking world. There has been an explosion of Napoleonic literature since the 1970s, deriving largely from the emergence of Europe from the Cold War. Tempered by a century of world wars, political and social change heavily influenced perspectives, from the traditional French hagiography to the Marxist indictments of Napoleon's betrayal of the French Revolution. American, British, and Australian historians have contributed critical and analytical accounts of armies, warfare, and society during this era. Although the French and British schools heavily influenced American scholars, they have also produced some of the most significant studies of Austrian and Prussian perspectives. Further, Australia has produced a number of historians who have contributed significantly to the historiography of both Britain and the coalition facing Napoleon. In Britain, historians have begun to depart from their worship of Wellington to an examination of his allies—with particular reference to Spain. Their exploration of Napoleonic Europe, too, has provided invaluable and comprehensive insight in the French Empire from both the French and European views.

The conclusion of the Cold War has profoundly altered the historiography of the Napoleonic Wars by offering a multipolar perspective of German princes, Italian states, and popular insurrections. A vast body of work has been produced on these subjects as narrative and quantitative studies. Finally, the post–Cold War era ushered in the age of the peace-dividend and a substantial military transformation in the United States and Europe. The nature of this change led to greater interest in historical examples of military transformations, including the Napoleonic Wars.

In 1986, almost in anticipation of these events, Peter Paret wrote in *Makers of Modern Strategy*—a new and revised volume of Edward Mead Earle's 1941 classic work—that the Napoleonic Wars introduced a Revolution in Military Affairs (RMA) on the same scale as the military revolution of the seventeenth century. This notion of an RMA centered on national conscription, logistics, and organization expanded the scope and nature of the Napoleonic Wars. This argument has been featured prominently in the last twenty years. Books and articles on Napoleonic conscription policies and their impact and implications on European society abound. The utility of using the RMA model, however, deserves greater examination.

An area of significant historiographical attention surrounds the question of the Peninsular War's impact on the Napoleonic Empire. Certainly, the plethora of histories on the conventional war in Spain established a school that argues the centrality of the Peninsular campaigns to the collapse of Napoleon's empire by denying the French absolute victory and draining imperial resources. The counterargument stipulates the role of the "Spanish ulcer," in diverting manpower and resources from central Europe, but disputes the thesis placing it as the central event. This is not simply the product of discourse between French and British historians, but German, Austrian, and Russian scholars have also joined the debate.

The historical dialogue, coupled with the emergence of "asymmetrical warfare" after the Second World War, and within the context of the post–Cold War era, has led to the emergence of vibrant scholarship on the role of guerrilla war, and popular insurrection in the Napoleonic Wars. Early explorations of this subject were limited to Spanish historians and the contributions of the guerrillas to Napoleon's defeat in Spain. In the late 1980s, however, this discussion expanded with British and American historians elaborating on Spanish scholarship and providing their own conclusions. Furthermore, research on popular revolts in Calabria (1806) and the Tyrol (1809) are appearing, bringing the central European focus increasingly into view. The history of popular revolts against Napoleonic rule is a recent addition to the historiography. It should not, however, be considered a separate topic in the realm of military history, but properly placed in a national and/or regional context. These histories are discussed as such in this book. This volume therefore serves as a guide to the changing nature of Napoleon historiography, looking at the most significant works and schools of thought while offering insight and critical questions. To that end, holes in the literature will become apparent, encouraging others to fill these gaps.

1 THE ORIGINS OF NAPOLEONIC WARFARE

I n 1986, Peter Paret wrote that the Napoleonic Era marked a "revolution in military affairs."[1] The term emerged during the last decades of the Cold War and has since been appropriated by military historians seeking to tie social, political, organizational, and technological change to military institutions, which resulted in dramatic or, more appropriately, decisive outcome. The Revolution in Military Affairs (RMA) in the twenty-first century has come to represent any perceived "revolutionary change" in warfare. Andrew Liaropoulos, "Revolutions in Warfare: Theoretical Paradigms and Historical Evidence" (2006), addressed the problem of applying this broad definition to virtually all areas of military history, including the French Revolutionary and Napoleonic Era. As this period of war witnessed the institution of conscription, the establishment of modern military organizations, mobilization of national resources,

1   Peter Paret, "Napoleon and the Revolution in War," in *Makers of Modern Strategy: From Machiavelli to the Nuclear Age*, ed. Peter Paret (Princeton, NJ: Princeton University Press, 1986), 123–42.

and the first decisive application of army operations resulting in complete victory over an enemy state, historians have often perceived this era as one of revolution. Combined with traditional interpretations of the French Revolutionary and Napoleonic Wars, the association of RMA with this period is logical. Revisionists, however, have argued persuasively that the RMA argument is overdone and too broad in its approach. Furthermore, the current historical trend is to place the wars within their historical context and, once done, question the extent to which the various changes actually constituted a revolution.

The question of evolution and revolution continues to permeate the historiography of the French Revolutionary and Napoleonic Wars. Virtually all historians of this period agree that Napoleon was not an originator but an innovator of forms of war developed before and during the Revolution. As Napoleon and many of his marshals and senior officers entered military service prior to 1789, the extent to which pre-1789 military reforms and theories impacted their understanding and conduct of war after 1789 remains central to the discussion of Napoleonic warfare. Until the 1990s, this question was squarely focused on the French military system, and historians incorrectly perceived eighteenth-century warfare as static and limited in scope, thereby failing to understand or cope with the new dynamic created by the Revolution and perpetuated by Napoleon. The past twenty years, however, have clearly illustrated the fallacy in earlier historical examinations.

Bourcet, Guibert, and Du Teil form the trinity of traditional perspectives on pre-1789 French military theories. Pierre de Bourcet's *Principes de la guerre de montagne* (1775), Jacques Antoine Hippolyte, Comte de Guibert's *Essai général de tactique*

(1772), and Jean du Teil's artillery theories on the application of massed batteries were written during the age of French military reforms in the decades following the Seven Years' War (1756–1763). In particular, these theorists advocated the operational use of combat divisions in the theater of war, the concentration of artillery on the battlefield as well as its establishment as an independent branch of the army, and the creation of light infantry to operate in skirmish order and the use of attack columns for shock as opposed to the traditional line formation. As progressive as their ideas were, they found little support among the senior leadership, and it was not until the Revolution that their operational and tactical concepts were applied. Spenser Wilkinson, *The French Army before Napoleon* (1915), and later Robert Quimby, *The Background of Napoleonic Warfare: The Theory of Military Tactics in Eighteenth-Century France* (1952), formed the cornerstone of traditional examinations of pre-revolutionary theories and their influence on French tactical reforms during the Revolution.

Wilkinson and Quimby influenced later historians such as David Chandler (1966), who wrote that Napoleon "saw more clearly than any other soldier of his generation the full potentialities of the French military doctrines."[2] Gunther E. Rothenberg, *The Art of Warfare in the Age of Napoleon* (1976), argued that while these theories existed pre-1789, their application during the Revolution constituted a new art of war. He believed, however, that these innovations could only be accomplished with the Revolution's political reforms and were not limited to Napoleon. Paddy Griffith, *The Art of War of Revolutionary*

2   David G. Chandler, *The Campaigns of Napoleon: The Mind and Method of History's Greatest Soldier* (New York: Macmillan, 1966), 136.

France, 1789–1802 (1998), concurred but elaborated on the point, stressing that the financial, organizational, and logistical limitations of French Revolutionary armies actually retarded their ability to apply these tactical theories appropriately. John A. Lynn explored the practical application of tactical doctrine in his now-classic *The Bayonets of the Republic: Motivation and Tactics in the Army of Revolutionary France, 1791–1794* (1984, reprinted in 1996). Despite the breadth of what his title implies, Lynn conducted a case study of the *Armée du Nord*, which operated in Belgium. It was one of at least ten French armies operating on the frontiers. Lynn concluded that the army's performance was inconsistent, but soldiers beginning as raw volunteers became experienced veterans who employed the new tactical doctrines over time.

Discussion of tactics becomes important to historical inquiry as the myth of French skirmishers in the thousands advancing before the vaunted massed attack columns of French divisions pervaded much of the general literature. The French myth of a national army of highly motivated volunteers adhering to revolutionary tactical doctrines began with the victory of the French at Valmy in 1792. Yet, it is clear that the advance of the serried ranks of the Prussians was conducted with apprehension, and the weight of the attack actually fell on the battalions of French regulars, as opposed to the volunteers who occupied the flanks.

Historians and independent scholars tend to examine the French military regulations of 1791, the *Reglément 1791*. It provides a clear statement on the "new" tactical drill for the French army of the Revolution. Unfortunately, too many historians believe that if it was in the drill manual, it was done in the field.

The regulations of 1791 illustrate the significance of pre-1789 theories, but clearly the application of those tactical doctrines was not uniformly employed until 1794–1795 and most likely 1796. Napoleonic tactics evolved from these theories and as a consequence of a decade of war and campaigning.

In terms of Napoleonic warfare, the issue comes to the fore because Napoleon's soldiers were largely professionals through 1812. His Grande Armée of 1805–1807 was perhaps the most experienced and best led in Europe. They were capable and often performed complex maneuvers on the battlefield, defeating Austrian, Prussian, and Russian armies over an eighteen-month period. Much of the tactical discussion, however, of the Napoleonic Era has focused on the issue of column versus line. In particular, this discussion centers on the question of why French tactical doctrine worked against the armies of central Europe, but failed largely when employed against the British. This discussion began with Sir Charles Oman, *Column and Line in the Peninsular War* (1910), and Sir John Fortescue, *A History of the British Army*, 13 vols. (1899–1930), and continued with Paddy Griffith. Although British victories over the French at Maida in 1806, in the Peninsular War, and at Waterloo are very clear, they have often warped our understanding of Napoleonic tactics, as case in point with Rory Muir, *Tactics and the Experience of Battle in the Age of Napoleon* (1998). Despite the title, Muir spends far more time examining Napoleonic warfare through Wellington's lenses. The book provides a clear understanding of the Anglo-French military experience but little of the continental campaigns. James Arnold, "A Reappraisal of Column Versus Line in the Peninsular War" (2004), sheds light on the impact Oman and Fortescue had on our understanding of British and

French tactics. He took Oman and subsequent Anglocentric historians to task, reexamining French tactics at Maida and providing alternative explanations for the failings of the French other than tactics.

The focus on the tactical debate of French and British narratives is a reflection of available sources, or more appropriately the language limitations of English-speaking historians. The authors of *Fighting Techniques of the Napoleonic Age, 1792–1815* (2008) present perhaps the best overview of the tactical developments during the Revolutionary and Napoleonic Era. Nonetheless, historical investigation into tactical developments in Prussia, Austria, and Russia is relatively new, with the exception of Peter Paret, *Yorck and the Era of Prussian Reform, 1807–1815* (1966), which examines organizational and tactical reforms in the Prussian army after the kingdom's humiliating defeat in 1806. His *Cognitive Challenge of War: Prussia 1806* (2009) is not particularly concerned with tactics and doctrine, but it does examine these issues in relation to Prussia's French opponents. Paret's ability to access German sources provides another window into the world of Napoleonic warfare beyond the standard French or British narratives.

Gunther E. Rothenberg provides a lucid discussion of Austria's response to French Revolutionary and Napoleonic tactics in *Napoleon's Great Adversaries: The Archduke Charles and the Austrian Army, 1792–1814* (1982), and pointed to political limitations restricting the adoption of the French system in Austria. Most recently, Robert Goetz, *1805, Austerlitz* (2005), looked specifically at Austrian and Russian tactics on the battlefield, making it abundantly clear that the fighting on December 2, 1805, was a hard-fought victory that was won by

Napoleon at the operational level, but the tactical engagements throughout the day indicated the professionalism of the Austrian and Russian troops. Lee Eysturlid, *The Formative Influences, Theories, and Campaigns of the Archduke Carl of Austria* (2000), places Austrian military thought in the context of the eighteenth century, very much in the manner by which Wilkinson et al. illustrated the continuity between theory and practice in the French army.

Beyond the tactical debate, historians have been keen to explore the state of the French army prior to and during the French Revolution to better understand the armies that Napoleon commanded in 1796 and thereafter. The general discussion begins with the premise that the French army, humiliated during the Seven Years' War, underwent substantial reform in the decades following defeat. The result of these reforms was a willingness to accept new doctrines and methods of waging war. Indeed, these reforms returned to the fundamentals of military education the technical branches of artillery and engineering—which were the hallmarks of French armies during the age of Louis XIV—and opened the officer corps to "men of talent." The argument continues that these reforms, combined with the reduction in the size of French armed forces, permitted a leaner institution. The performance of the French army in the American Revolution certainly enhances this perspective. Finally, the ability of the French army to adapt to the Revolution and achieve significant military victories in the first years of war reinforces it.

A good number of historians have explored this subject. Sam Scott produced two important works on the army during this period: *From Yorktown to Valmy* (1998) and *The Response of the Royal Army to the French Revolution* (1978). David Bien contributed a seminal article on the subject, "The Army in the French Enlightenment: Reform, Reaction and Revolution" (1979), and the eminent historian Harold T. Parker, "Napoleon and French Army Values" (1991), examined the influence of traditional French military honor on Napoleon and his contemporaries. The extent to which traditional rather than revolutionary values influenced military culture can be found in John Lynn, "Toward an Army of Honor" (1989). Owen Connelly challenged Lynn's argument in a lively debate sparked by Lynn's article in a forum on the French army from 1789 to 1815 published in *French Historical Studies* (1989).

Perhaps the best comprehensive history of the French Revolutionary armies and their impact on Napoleonic generalship is Ramsay Weston Phipps, *The Armies of the First French Republic and the Rise of the Marshals of Napoleon I*, 5 vols. (1926–1935). Phipps details the campaigns of the respective French armies during the course of the wars of the First and Second Coalitions, and the role played by those revolutionary officers who would become the marshalate of Napoleon's empire. The volumes are required reading for any student of the Napoleonic Wars, but they are at times rather dense. Nevertheless, any serious study aimed at understanding the school of war from which French armies and leaders graduated must read Phipps.

The best works on the political and institutional climate in which the French armies emerged, are Jean-Paul Bertaud, *The Army of the French Revolution* (1988), Alan Forrest, *The Soldiers of the French Revolution* (1990), and Howard Brown, *War, Revolution, and the Bureaucratic State* (1995). The English translation of Bertaud's book is quite good, although footnotes were not included. Forrest is concerned with the political education of the army, while Brown traces the institutional evolution of the Ministry of War, eventually run by Lazare Carnot and inherited by Napoleon in 1799. Lynn's *Bayonets of the Republic*, mentioned earlier in this chapter, should also be consulted.

The origins of Napoleonic warfare can clearly be seen in Napoleon's first command as general in chief of the army of Italy. The campaign in 1796–1797 introduced Napoleon as the talented, young, dynamic and charismatic general of Revolutionary France. He joined the ranks of the already well-known Jean-Baptiste Jourdan and Lazare Hoche. Napoleon's campaign in 1796–1797 is explored well in David Chandler, *The Campaigns of Napoleon* (1966), and more thoroughly in Phipps, *The Army of Italy, 1796 to 1797*, vol. 4 (1935). The success of the campaign, and its role in catapulting Napoleon to the top of the military ladder in France, resulted in a number of histories that question the extent to which Napoleon's plans and actions were his own. By the late nineteenth century French military histories, specifically Leoncé Krebs and Henri Maurice, *Les Campagne dans les Alpes pendant la Révolution*, 2 vols. (1891), provided clear evidence that Lazare Carnot, minister of war, issued very detailed orders specifying the nature of Napoleon's offensive into Piedmont and subsequently the direction he should take in the offensive against the Austrians in Lombardy. Spenser Wilkinson produced two books examining the origins and conduct of the campaign in Italy: *The Defence of Piedmont, 1742–1748: A Prelude to the Study of Napoleon* (1927) and *The Rise of General Bonaparte* (1930). The former is concerned with the campaign of French marshal Jean-Baptiste Francois des Marets, marquis de Maillebois, and his chief of staff, Gen. Pierre Bourcet, in Piedmont during the War of Austrian Succession (1740–1748). Wilkinson believed Napoleon used the same strategy to achieve victory in 1796.

Napoleon's more recent critics include Owen Connelly, *Blundering to Glory* (1987), who argued that Napoleon's subordinates and the incompetence of his Austrian opponents won the victory. Connelly's thesis received strength from Italian historian Guglielmo Ferrero, *The Gamble: Bonaparte in Italy, 1796–1797* (English translation 1961). Ferrero believed much of the Napoleonic legend surrounding the campaign was manufactured first by Bonapartists and then French nationalists. He presented evidence that the French and Piedmontese were in secret negotiations for that state's withdrawal from the coalition, and the French offensive provided cover for the diplomatic maneuver. He equally stressed that Napoleon's operations in Italy were not as brilliant and far more brutal than previously presented. To Ferrero, Italy was the true victim of French aggression and Austrian duplicity.

The study of French armies during the Revolution is only part of the process in understanding the context of the Napoleonic Wars. The Napoleonic Wars did not occur in a vacuum. The diplomatic and political state of Europe produced several small wars in the decades following the general European conflagration of the Seven Years' War (1756–1763), the American Revolution (1777–1783), the War of the Bavarian Succession (1778–1779), the Austro-Russian-Ottoman War (1787–1791), and the almost Austro-Prussian War of 1790.[3] T. C. W. Blanning, *The Origins of the French Revolutionary Wars* (1986) and *The*

3   The date of the American Revolution is listed from French declaration of war on the British, not the beginning of American rebellion, which was 1775. The Austrians and Prussians mobilized their armies and almost came to blows in 1790. The war was avoided with the death of Joseph II and the accession of Leopold II.

French Revolutionary Wars, 1787–1802 (1996), Gunther E. Rothenberg, "The Origins, Causes and Extensions of the Wars of the French Revolution and Napoleon" (1988), and Michael Hochedlinger, "Who's Afraid of the French Revolution" (2003), have all successfully placed the wars of the French Revolution in the context of Europe in 1789. The French Revolutionary Wars occurred within the increasing competitive nature of European politics, which had never truly quieted since 1763.

In 2007, historian David Bell published *The First Total War*, which received significant press and sales but was attacked by military historians, particularly those who specialized in the French Revolutionary and Napoleonic Wars. Bell argued that "the intellectual transformations of the Enlightenment, followed by the political fermentation of 1789–1792 produced new understandings of war that made possible the cataclysmic intensification of the fighting over the next twenty-three years of war. . . . This is a new argument."[4] It was, in fact, not a new argument and one that ignored the historical literature of the 1990s. The argument was predicated upon the acceptance of warfare prior to 1789 as one of limited political and military objectives and resources. In terms of military historiography, Bell's thesis created a firestorm because it received much attention but ran counter to the current state of military historiography of the eighteenth and nineteenth centuries. The notion that the eighteenth century witnessed limited wars was successfully challenged by Jeremy Black, "Eighteenth Century Warfare Reconsidered" (1994), and more recently Franz Szabo, *The Seven Years War in Europe, 1756–1763* (2008). Furthermore, the current trend to

4   David A. Bell, *The First Total War: Napoleon's Europe and the Birth of Warfare As We Know It* (New York: Houghton Mifflin, 2007), 9.

examine the global history of the period in terms of European warfare in the colonial world suggests that the concept of "total war" related to resources, dynamics of warfare, and absolute victory was already understood and pursued. For example the genocidal Spanish response to the rebellion of Túpac Amaru in Mexico during the second half of the eighteenth century was examined in J. H. Elliott, *Empires of the Atlantic World: Britain and Spain in America, 1492–1830* (2006), among others. Finally, Bell's argument assumes that the ideological motivation superseded traditional goals in the French declaration and pursuit of war. It also assumes France's enemies perceived the French war as requiring a new social and political response. In fact, this was not the case, and was rejected earlier by Michael Hochedlinger, "Who's Afraid of the French Revolution" (2003). Moreover, according to the eminent diplomatic historian Paul Schroeder, *The Transformation of European Politics, 1763–1848* (1994), the only substantive change to come out of the war was the development of a new, or modified, international system.

One of the historical facts often overlooked by students of Napoleonic history is the overlap of the War of the Second Coalition and the Napoleonic Wars. The expedition to Egypt in 1798 was conducted with the purposeful intent of striking at British interests in the eastern Mediterranean. Nathan Schur, *Napoleon in the Holy Land* (2006), is the most recent discussion, and Virginia Aksan, *Ottoman Wars 1700–1870* (2007), looks at the invasion from the Turkish perspective. Juan Cole's *Napoleon's Egypt: Invading the Middle East* (2007) is more polemic, interpreting the French invasion as the beginning of European imperialism. An interesting French perspective available in English is Joseph-Marie Moiret's *The Memoirs of Napoleon's Egyptian*

Expedition (2006). Perhaps the best primary source is *Napoleon in Egypt: Al-Jabarti's Chronicle of the First Seven Months of the French Occupation* (2003). It is the translation of an Egyptian contemporary and has been a standard source on the invasion. Napoleon's campaign in the Middle East did much to boost his reputation. He left the French army in Egypt in 1799 and returned to France to participate in the plot to overthrow the Directory.

Napoleon inherited the War of the Second Coalition (1798–1802) upon his assumption of power after November 1799. His famed Marengo campaign in June 1800 was conducted to regain the initiative in the failing war against the Second Coalition. James Arnold, *Marengo and Hohenlinden* (2005); Phipps, *The Armies of the First French Republic and the Rise of the Marshals of Napoleon I*, vol. 5; and A. B. Rodger, *The War of the Second Coalition, 1798–1801* (1964) all examine the war from revolutionary to Napoleonic. Napoleon's narrowly won victory at Marengo, however, led only to a six-month cession of hostilities. General Moreau's victory over the Austrians at Hohenlinden in Germany in December 1800 was the deathblow to the Habsburg cause and a coalition that fell apart long before that date. Paul Schroeder's article, "The Collapse of the Second Coalition" (1987), does well to explain the essential failures of anti-French coalitions.

The Treaty of Lunéville, which ended the war with Austria in February 1801, and the Peace of Amiens a year later, which concluded the war with Britain, followed the coup d'état of 18 Brumaire that brought Napoleon to power. The period of the Consulate (1800–1804) is still technically part of the history of the First French Republic, yet Napoleon's domestic and foreign policies clearly place those intervening years between the wars as an era of transition. Historians locate Napoleon's 1800 campaign in the Revolutionary Wars, while interpreting events after 1801, as entirely "Napoleonic," meaning the course taken by France and the ultimate outbreak of European war was the sole responsibility of the French consul and soon-to-be emperor.

Charles Esdaile's *Napoleon's Wars* (2007) and Paul Schroeder's *Transformation of European Politics* (1994) argue that despite the events of the French Revolutionary Wars, Napoleon is squarely to blame for the wars' origins in 1803. Esdaile traces Napoleon's career through the Revolution, pointing out events of Napoleon's own making and his desire to act against the wishes and intent of the revolutionary government. Schroeder argues that Napoleon rejected international agreements and agitated Europe to war in 1803 and thereafter. Rothenberg, too, believed that "France inevitably would have raised up a paramount military figure, but all we know of Napoleon's most competent rivals—Jourdan, Hoche, and Moreau—suggests that if they had gained power, French political ambitions would have been more modest."[5] Frederick Kagan wrote that "the Peace of 1801–1802 put the powder in the bomb; Napoleon lit the fuse."[6]

Of course exploring the question of whether France would have pursued a Napoleonic course without Napoleon is counterfactual history, but there are two points of interest to the historical traveler. The first concerns the Peace of Campo Formio (1797) that concluded the War of the First Coalition, and the second relates to an interpretation that requires the French to

5   Gunther E. Rothenberg, *The Napoleonic Wars* (London: Cassell, 1999), 34.

6   Frederick Kagan, *The End of the Old Order: Napoleon and Europe, 1801–1805* (Philadelphia: Da Capo Press, 2005), 28.

hold the diplomatic initiative. To the latter point, the discourse on the origins of the Napoleonic Wars begins with the violation of the Treaty of Lunéville (1801) with the annexation of Piedmont in 1802, followed in 1803 by Napoleon's refusal to abide by the articles of the Treaty of Amiens with Great Britain—although Britain refused to abide by their agreements, too. It assumes that without Napoleon, meaning with a moderate French government instead, the Austrians, Russians, and British would have accepted the treaties. In terms of Campo Formio, the agreement was fully accepted by the French revolutionary government, despite its being dictated by Napoleon. The Treaty of Lunéville established between France and Austria simply reaffirmed the agreement of Campo Formio. The problem is that Austria found Campo Formio reprehensible, and Johann Amadeus Franz de Paula, Baron of Thugut, the Austrian chancellor at the time, only accepted it as a temporary accord. To that end, the acceptance of Lunéville was done under duress. This is the view of Karl Roider, *Baron Thugut and Austria's Response to the French Revolution* (1987). If one agrees that a moderate French government in 1801 would have signed Lunéville and subsequently Amiens, would Austria, Russia, and Britain have been willing to live with the limitations on their respective powers?

The question can be answered by examining some of the central goals of the Third Coalition, formed in 1805 against Napoleonic France. The Austrians and Russians sought the restoration of the King of Sardinia to Piedmont and the independence of Genoa. The Russians further desired that the princes of the Holy Roman Empire retain the independence they received from certain restrictions after the Imperial Recess in 1803. Russia played a significant role in the negotiations prior to the recess, and Tsar Alexander's mother was the daughter of the ruler of Württemberg. Assuming a moderate French government sat in Paris, the annexation of Piedmont and Genoa in 1802 would probably not have occurred. For Britain the issue remains unclear, as Prime Minister Henry Addington was perfectly willing to come to terms with the French in 1802, but previous prime minister William Pitt was reluctant during the initial phase of negotiations in 1801. A general discussion of British concerns during this period, 1793–1805, can be found in Jeremy Black's essay, "British Strategy and the Struggle with France, 1793–1815" (2008). In short, a continental peace after 1801 was possible only with the honoring of the Treaty of Lunéville. British actions, however, were completely dependent on whether they could trust the French government, regardless of whether it was under Napoleon or someone else.

2   THE NAPOLEONIC WARS

In the beginning, there is David Chandler. Students of the Napoleonic Wars—past, present, and future—should begin their studies with Chandler's monumental *The Campaigns of Napoleon: The Mind and Method of History's Greatest Soldier*. Published in 1966, *The Campaigns of Napoleon* returned the Napoleonic Wars to the center stage of military history. Brilliantly written and well-researched, the impressive single-volume, thousand-plus-page history popularized Napoleon's campaigns, inspiring a new generation of students and scholars. The book remains the standard narrative after more than forty years. Chandler, however, is only the beginning, as his history is concerned solely with those campaigns between 1796 and 1815 that directly involved Napoleon. Indeed, there is no chapter devoted to Spain after Napoleon departed in January 1809, and minimal space is given to the secondary theaters of war during his campaigns in central Europe and Russia. Chandler's discussion of Napoleon's allies is limited, and his perspective is restricted to French and British sources. These shortcomings do not invalidate his examination of campaigns in Germany, Austria, and Russia, but they do shape his narrative and analysis. In the four and a half decades since its publication, there has been an explosion of material readily available in Spanish, German, Italian, and Russian, providing for fuller perspectives of Napoleon's enemies.

Since Chandler, Charles Esdaile, *The Wars of Napoleon* (1995), and David Gates, *The Napoleonic Wars, 1803–1815* (1997), have appeared. Both Esdaile and Gates are historians of the Peninsular War (1808–1814) and approach the Napoleonic Wars from a decidedly Anglocentric view. Although Chandler was a British historian, his understanding of the wars beyond Spain in 1808 and Belgium 1815 is interpreted exclusively through French lenses. In fact, the differences between the interpretive schools are immediately quite significant and rather similar in a broader historiographical context.

A divide exists among Napoleonic historians as to whether the wars in central and eastern Europe rather than the Peninsular War (Spain and Portugal) represent the standard for understanding the Napoleonic Wars. The historians who favored the former dominated the historiography until the 1980s. Chandler and his predecessors focused almost exclusively on the campaigns against Austria, Prussia, and Russia. Their belief that the war in Spain (1808–1814) was largely a "sideshow" was the logical conclusion if the Napoleonic Wars were only understood by those campaigns in which Napoleon directly participated. Hence, Napoleon spent only four months in Spain, October 1808 through January 1809, and thereafter his brother Joseph and a variety of French marshals conducted the war in the Iberian Peninsula. A lively and active scholarship by more recent historians of the Peninsular War has since challenged this conventional approach. Even so, the Peninsular historians initially limited themselves to French and British sources until Esdaile and Gates. (See chapter on Peninsular War.) This perspective significantly influences their general histories of the Napoleonic Wars.

Although the ubiquitous comment that history is written by the victors applies in most cases, the French produced the largest number of histories and memoirs immediately following the conflict and throughout the nineteenth century. Histories of the wars written in English in the early twentieth century were substantially influenced by the French view and heavily shaped the interpretation of future historians such as Chandler. Much of his understanding of Napoleon's art of war was drawn from Gen. Hubert Camon's four books, *La guerre Napoléonienne: Les systèmes d'opération* (1907), *La guerre Napoléonienne: Précis des campagnes* (1925), *Quand et comment Napoléon a conçu son système de manœuvre* (1931), and *Quand et conçu Napoléon son système de bataille* (1935). Camon's analysis of Napoleonic warfare was clearly shaped during the fin de siècle and by the static nature of the First World War.

F. Loraine Petre wrote the second series of histories that influenced Chandler and remains required reading. An officer in the British army prior to the First World War, Petre produced five separate volumes on the campaigns in central Europe: *Napoleon's Campaign in Poland, 1806–1807* (1901); *Napoleon's Conquest of Prussia, 1806* (1907); *Napoleon and the Archduke Charles* (1909); *Napoleon's Last Campaign in Germany, 1813* (1912); and *Napoleon at Bay, 1814* (1913). Petre's narrative is terse and at times rather confusing, yet he relies extensively on German sources and utilizes archival material from the Service

Historique de l'Armée de Terre at Vincennes. The use of this archive had previously been limited to those histories produced in French, by the French army historical office, or to retired officers with regular access to the archives. As well, Petre included some discussion of the secondary theaters. He purposely shied from writing campaign history related to 1805, 1812, and 1815, which, he argued, were well covered and did not require another book. It was his intention to provide histories of the lesser-known campaigns for the English-speaking world.

In all, the essential dynamic of Napoleonic warfare was Napoleon's genius. The system worked well enough but failed without Napoleon. Thus, many of the early histories of the Napoleonic Wars, later examined by Chandler, focus on Napoleon's campaigns. They spent little, if any, time on the campaigns and theaters of war in which Napoleon made no appearance. Of course, this warped later appreciation and understanding of the dynamics of the Napoleonic Wars and did not adequately explain the reason for his defeat, other than personal failure. Much of this historiographical school, then, accepted the Napoleonic legend. French power was tied inexorably to the man, and the decline of the man meant the decline of French power. In this perspective, there is no room for factors beyond Napoleon and no room for a learning curve among Napoleon's enemies in terms of military organization, generalship, and quality of army. Indeed, there is no room for economic, social, and cultural analysis. The "great man" school dominated historical interpretation prior to World War II, and "gentlemen scholars" in Britain produced the body of Napoleonic military history. In France, too, both active and retired officers wrote the histories. Their understanding was decidedly shaped by the traditional interpretation that historical events were the product of individual action.

The emergence of the Annales School after 1945 led to a revisionist response to historical interpretation in general, but it did not impact Napoleonic military history until the 1970s.[1] Thus, Chandler could write *The Campaigns of Napoleon* without consideration of the revisionists. What began to emerge, however, were histories of the Napoleonic Wars that questioned the extent of Napoleon's genius, and an exclusively French narrative. Furthermore, the emphasis on Napoleon's genius allowed historians to ignore military systems. In many cases, this was a product of the narrative approach of the "drum and bugle" school of military history. A study of military systems did not appear in the field until the great "military revolution debate" surrounding the early modern era, inaugurated by Michael Roberts in 1956. The military histories of the Napoleonic Wars subsequently addressed the questions of genius and systems.

Gunther E. Rothenberg, *The Art of Warfare in the Age of Napoleon* (1976), examines the Napoleonic Wars as revolution, rather than evolution, in warfare. He believed the French levée en masse and Napoleon's conscription system, military organization, and the decisive nature of Napoleonic warfare represented a new era in warfare. He repeated this notion in *The Napoleonic Wars* (1999). Rothenberg examined Napoleon's enemies—the Austrians, Prussians, and Russians—with equal interest, integrating substantial German sources and providing a detailed

---

1   For a discussion of the response of the Annales School to military history see Peter Paret, "The Annales School and the History of War," *Journal of Military History* 73, no. 4 (October 2009): 1289–94.

account of coalition armies and generals. His discussion favored a systemic and institutional approach to an analysis of generalship.

Rothenberg did not question Napoleon's genius, but he rejected the notion that if Napoleon were a genius, then his opponents were incompetent. Although incompetent generalship appeared in several Napoleonic campaigns, it does not properly explain Napoleon's victories. *Art of Warfare* is essentially an institutional history, not a campaign narrative, therefore the structure, operations, and strategy of coalition armies is presented in a clearer and more concise manner, correcting some of Chandler's assessments drawn from limited sources. Rothenberg thus offers readers an accessible and broad view of the period. It remains a vital book for the uninitiated and a valuable reference for the scholar.

While Rothenberg provided wider context, Owen Connelly made a direct assault upon the Napoleonic legend in *Blundering to Glory: Napoleon's Military Campaigns* (1987). Connelly challenged the entire concept of Napoleon's genius. He argued that Napoleon's victories were more properly the product of luck, outstanding subordinates, and the mistakes of his enemies. Connelly conceded that Napoleon possessed talent and leadership, but in his analysis of Napoleon's campaigns, the luster is removed from the brilliance. The intention of the book is to attack the myth and compel the reader to consider factors beyond the person. Connelly did not draw his inspiration from the Annales School's attack on the individual in history, but he instead takes a traditional approach, seeking to critique the campaigns with a purposeful eye toward pointing out Napoleon's errors. Like Rothenberg, Connelly benefits from the use of German sources and is able to access Austrian and Prussian accounts of the campaigns.

Connelly does not address military systems, focusing exclusively on generalship. His book received criticism from Napoleonic historians who argued that he made too much of "blundering," but within its historiographical context, the book serves a very important purpose: challenging the "genius" thesis.

Jonathan Riley joined the fray, attacking the notion of Napoleonic genius in *Napoleon as a General: Command from the Battlefield to Grand Strategy* (2007). His examination of Napoleon as a general takes a thematic approach. Although Riley recognizes the French emperor's skill as army leader, he rejects the idea of Napoleon as a successful strategic thinker, instead theorizing that the emperor's failure to establish tangible strategic goals led to his inability to preserve his empire.

Charles Esdaile, *The Wars of Napoleon* (1995) and *The Napoleonic Wars* (2007), and David Gates, *The Napoleonic Wars, 1803–1815* (1997), produced the most comprehensive accounts of the Napoleonic Wars in the decades since Chandler. In the case of the latter, Gates rejects the genius of Napoleon but refuses to go to Connelly's extreme. He accepts Napoleon's talent as a military commander but, as with Rothenberg, considers military systems a fundamental factor in victory. To that end, the actions of the military commander's enemies are central to the outcome of events. For Gates, the Napoleonic Wars introduced a new age in warfare, and a portent of things to come. While balanced as far as genius and systems, Gates remains decidedly influenced by the British view, remarking that "two of the most celebrated battles in history occurred in this conflict: Trafalgar and Waterloo."[2] The Austrians and Russians benefited

---

2   David Gates, *The Napoleonic War, 1803–1815* (London: Arnold, 1997), xvii.

little from Trafalgar in 1805, their armies crushed by Napoleon at Austerlitz six weeks later. Though the Prussians would agree to Waterloo, there is a clear acceptance by Napoleonic historians that Waterloo was irrelevant in the sense that a French victory on that day would not have saved Napoleon from the armies of Austria and Russia in 1815.

Foremost among the revisionists is Charles Esdaile, who has attempted to single-handedly rewrite much of the history of the Napoleonic Wars. Napoleon appears center stage, as Esdaile, *The Wars of Napoleon* (1995), argues that without Napoleon, the chance of war between 1803–1815 was rather small. In the broader sense, placing the wars in historical context is important, but it cannot explain the continued conflict between France and Europe after the central issues of these wars were addressed and accepted. Esdaile is not concerned about systems or genius but rather the nature of the wars and their impact on Europe. He takes a much broader view of the era, examining popular resistance, occupation policies, and failures of Napoleonic policy. Esdaile's history is less concerned with military affairs than with their impact on European society and politics.

The publication of Esdaile's *The Napoleonic Wars: An International History, 1803–1815* (2007) casts his earlier discussions into an even broader light, by exploring the impact of the Napoleonic Wars on Europe and the overseas empires. In the decade following his first book, the post–Cold War era witnessed an explosion of "transnational" histories, seeking to link the events in Europe with those of Latin America, Southeast Asia, Africa, and the Middle East. Jeremy Black founded this historiographical movement in the world of European military history. Esdaile rejects the Napoleonic Wars as the end of an era but, with Rothenberg and Gates, views it as a break with the past in terms of scope and dynamic. By broadening his historical lens, Esdaile modified his earlier notion that Europe would not have experienced war in this era without Napoleon. European states, he argues, pursued their individual interests in terms of their relation with France, and those areas completely unrelated to France. Russia's wars with the Swedes (1808) and Ottomans (1806–1812) serve as two examples.

A recent examination of the Napoleonic Wars appeared in a special issue of the *Journal of Strategic Studies* in August 2008, in a series of articles titled "Re-assessing the Napoleonic Wars." Charles Esdaile, Jeremy Black, Frederick Schneid, and Philip Dwyer examine the extent to which Napoleon, Britain, and the continental powers employed strategy during the wars. Integrating recent histories, the special issue—taken as a whole—provides insight into the current historiographical debates. In particular, Esdaile and Schneid disagree on the extent to which Napoleon possessed a grand strategy. Esdaile sees Napoleon as an opportunist whose actions indicate a lack of an articulated strategy. Schneid believes the cultivation of satellite and client states revealed a coherent strategic vision. True to his global perspectives, Black explores the limitations imposed upon British strategy by its need to protect its colonial possessions. Philip Dwyer argues that the eighteenth-century mentality of coalitions failed to stem Napoleonic ambitions, and after 1812 a new understanding necessitating a balance between cooperation and individual interest dominated coalition strategy. Regardless of perspective, all of these essays reveal that recent historians have rejected the monolithic "genius" thesis in favor of a more complex analysis of Napoleon and the wars.

3 THE CAMPAIGNS

T he number of military histories of the Napoleonic Wars is quite extensive. They range from operational and tactical narratives to strategic analyses. The majority of the histories take a decidedly French view, with the exception of those concerned with the Peninsular War or Waterloo Campaign. These two topics have received significant coverage from the British perspective. It is only in the past three decades that Austrian, Prussian, and Russian perspectives have made their way into the historical narrative. Much of this has to do with available sources and documents, and with a desire of historians to approach the subjects from these alternative views. In general, there remains much work to do to present new perspectives and narratives. This chapter is not concerned with the broad histories as seen in Chandler, Gates, and Esdaile. Those books were discussed earlier. The focus of this chapter is the history of the specific campaigns fought between 1805 and 1815.

The starting point for a detailed study of the respective campaigns is always David Chandler. The caveat, however, is the limitation of his sources, as Chandler did not examine German or Russian histories. After Chandler, one must consult the classic campaign histories of F. Loraine Petre. Petre's histories are individual, detailed studies of the campaigns of 1806, 1807, 1809, 1813, and 1814. Petre explained that his desire was to explore those campaigns not as well known as Austerlitz (1805) and Waterloo (1815). Furthermore, the state of British military history at the time of writing was decidedly focused on the Peninsular War. An introduction to Petre's interpretations of the Napoleonic Wars is Albert Nofi, *Napoleon at War: Selected Writings of F. Loraine Petre* (1984). These histories are critical because they provide a detailed analysis and equal time to the allied armies. The greatest drawback to Petre is the terse narrative. It is often difficult to follow, but the result is a solid understanding of events, decisions, and outcomes.

The War of the Third Coalition (1803–1805) witnessed Napoleon's greatest victory at Austerlitz. The preponderance of the histories of this war have been drawn from French sources. The Austrians produced no official history of the campaign, and only two substantial articles appeared in Austria in the late nineteenth century dealing with this subject. The Russians produced a bit but tended to focus on 1812 rather than 1805. The first significant English coverage of this battle was Christopher Duffy, *Austerlitz 1805* (1977). The book provides a lucid overall examination of the formation of the Third Coalition and the strategy and operations of the respective armies in the main theater of war, south Germany and Austria. Duffy provides a careful analysis of the battle and the operational decisions made by Napoleon, Tsar Alexander I, and Gen. Franz Von Weyrother, who was responsible for allied war plans. Duffy spends some time on tactics but focuses largely on the divisional level.

The most thorough tactical exploration of the battle is Robert Goetz, *1805, Austerlitz* (2005). Goetz utilizes Austrian and Russian sources to provide a full account of the nature of the battle. Unlike in Duffy, where corps and divisions move as ordered in a choreographed fashion, Goetz's history is more concerned with the specifics of the tactical engagements. His book portrays the battle as a series of disjointed engagements that when combined created the larger events and conditions that led to French victory and allied defeat. The failures of the Russian and Austrian command structures loom large here, although their prowess at the regimental and battalion level is on par with their French opponents.

Two other books published in 2005 for the bicentennial of the Napoleonic Wars are Frederick W. Kagan, *The End of the Old Order: Napoleon and Europe, 1801–1805*, and Frederick C. Schneid, *Napoleon's Conquest of Europe: The War of the Third Coalition*. They view the campaign as a culmination of political and diplomatic events in Europe from 1801 to 1805. Kagan framed the coming of war and the rise of Napoleonic France in closer terms to the changing nature of twenty-first-century events, "rogue states," and aggressive foreign policy. He consulted French and Austrian archives and produced a broad account of the war. Schneid saw the war and its context as continuity in European affairs since the eighteenth century. His account moves from the diplomatic and grand strategic situation of the participants to the decisions on the battlefield of Austerlitz, with particular discussion of the subsidiary theaters of war.

The accounts of the War of the Third Coalition all do well to provide the general plans of the respective powers, but in the discussion of the campaign most focus on the main theater of war in central Europe. The 1805 campaign also involved military operations in the Italian peninsula. In 1805 Marshal André Massena and the Archduke Charles of Austria, conducted a brief campaign culminating in the battle of Caldiero. Events in Italy in 1805 are covered in full in Schneid, *Napoleon's Conquest of Europe*, and Schneid, *Napoleon's Italian Campaigns, 1805–1815* (2002). The consequences for the kingdom of Naples, a member of the coalition against France, are also explored in William Flayhart, *Counterpoint to Trafalgar* (1992), and Milton Finley, *The Most Monstrous of Wars* (1994). The former is a very good account of the role played by the Neapolitan kingdom in the Third Coalition and the failed Anglo-Russian expedition to Italy in 1805–1806. The latter book explores the bloody five-year guerrilla war in Naples following the French conquest.

A year passed between the end of the War of the Third Coalition and the conquest of Prussia in 1806. During that intervening period, Prussia joined a French alliance and then—after being duped by Napoleon—went to war with France in the autumn of 1806. The Prussian campaign has received a great deal of attention from German historians, and historians of Prussia who view the rapid collapse of the militarized kingdom as a metaphor for the end of the Old Regime. Most recently the eminent historian Peter Paret published *The Cognitive Challenge of War: Prussia 1806* (2009), in which he addresses the social and intellectual implications of Prussia's defeat. Dennis Showalter, the master of German military history, produced two outstanding articles on the Prussian army's development from the end of the Seven Years' War to Waterloo: "Hubertusberg to Auerstädt: The Prussian Army in Decline?" (1994) and "Reform and Stability: Prussia's Military Dialectic From Hubertusberg to Waterloo" (forthcoming). In both, Showalter argues that there was nothing wrong with the Prussian army in the late eighteenth century. Its armies performed better than any other in the First Coalition. The problem, essentially, in 1806 was that the French out-Prussianed the Prussians. Napoleon's army was larger and as good, if not better, than the Prussians on the battlefield. The collapse of the state after the military defeat was a separate matter.

There are several books available on 1806 from the French perspective. F. N. Maude, *The Jena Campaign, 1806* (1909, reprinted in 1998), and *Napoleon's Finest: Davout and His 3rd Corps, Combat Journal of Operations, 1805–1807* (2006) are quite good. The latter book is an edited and annotated reprint of Marshal Louis N. Davout, *Operations du IIIe Corps, 1806– 1807* (1896). This primary source is invaluable for students of military history. The translation and reprint has been well received, although it is difficult to find and expensive. Unfortunately, only French archival documents on this campaign remain. Much of the Prussian military archive on 1806 was destroyed during the Second World War. This makes any future balanced history a challenge for historians.

The rapid defeat of the Prussian army on October 14 did not lead to the conclusion of the war. Frederick William III, King of Prussia, and Tsar Alexander I signed a military agreement, effectively establishing the Fourth Coalition against Napoleon. The Russian armies, however, were still assembling in eastern Poland when the Prussians fought at Jena-Auerstädt.

French armies advanced on Berlin and into Prussian Poland to take up position for winter quarters, expecting to deal with the Russians in the spring. Events, however, dictated otherwise, and an unintended early campaign in Poland resulted in some of the bloodiest fighting of the Napoleonic Wars.

If there are few books on the campaigns of 1806, even less exist on the campaign in Poland, 1806–1807. Petre remains the standard work, although James R. Arnold and Ralph R. Reinertsen, *Crisis in the Snows: Russia Confronts Napoleon: The Eylau Campaign 1806–1807* (2007), is the most recent. The winter campaign in Poland gave Napoleon his first battlefield rebuff at Eylau, followed in June, with one of his greatest victories at Friedland. Nonetheless, historians have not explored this campaign in any great detail, although its ramifications on the French army were enormous. Two years of campaigning, and the losses suffered in January and February, required Napoleon to pour tens of thousands of conscripts into the Grande Armée. The result was that the French army in 1807 and thereafter was significantly different to the armies Napoleon commanded in 1805 and 1806.

Although campaign histories are lacking for 1807, there is a great deal available on 1809. The Austrian war in 1809 tested the resolve of Napoleon's grand empire and the extent to which the military reforms of the Archduke Charles, generalissimus of the Austrian army, succeeded. Until recently, Petre's single-volume history remained the standard work. John H. Gill's three-volume history of 1809, *1809: Thunder on the Danube: Napoleon's Defeat of the Habsburgs* (2008–2010), is now the most important. Gill presents an incredibly balanced synthesis and analysis of the campaign. He provides details on French and Austrian strategy, operations, logistics, and politics. He utilizes sources in French, German, Italian, and English, as well as consulting French and Austrian military archives. Gill's history provides ample coverage of the secondary theaters in Italy, Germany, and Poland, as well as the revolt in the Tyrol and counterinsurgency operations conducted by Bavarian and Italian troops.

Gunther E. Rothenberg, the foremost historian of the Austrian army, examined the campaign from an institutional and strategic perspective in *Napoleon's Great Adversary: The Archduke Charles and the Austrian Army, 1792–1814* (1982). In 2004, he published his final book, *The Emperor's Last Victory*, which focused solely on 1809. Rothenberg was the leading expert on the battle of Wagram, and the latter book is extremely thorough in examining both Napoleon's preparation and crossing of the Danube, and the archduke's handling of the army during the climactic battle.

The campaign of 1809 is also notable for the Austrian adoption of the French organizational system, and the integration of several operational and tactical principles. Rothenberg addresses these in *Napoleon's Great Adversary*, but Robert Epstein, *Napoleon's Last Victory and the Emergence of Modern War* (1994), interprets Napoleon's ability to coordinate the movement of armies from multiple theaters to a single point (Vienna), as the beginning of modern war. This challenged the prevailing notion that the 1813 campaign served as the school for modern warfare as observed by Helmuth von Moltke the Elder, chief of staff of the Prussian army during the Wars of German Unification.

The Franco-Austrian War also witnessed extensive operations by Napoleon's *Rheinbund*, or Confederation of the Rhine, allies and his army of the Kingdom of Italy. The participation of German troops was covered thoroughly in John H. Gill, *With Eagles to Glory* (1992). The Italian campaign of 1809 and subsequent operations of the army of Italy in Hungary and at Wagram are explored in Frederick C. Schneid, *Napoleon's Italian Campaigns* (2002). The war also witnessed popular revolts against the Napoleonic order in the Tyrol and Germany. F. Gunther Eyck, *Loyal Rebels* (1986), introduced the pro-Habsburg rebellion, led by Andreas Hofer, in the former Austrian Tyrol to an English-speaking audience. Hofer's revolt was in a broad sense anti-Napoleonic, but its immediate target was the Bavarian regime, which annexed the Tyrol in 1806 as a reward for its alliance with France the previous year. The potential for a larger revolt occurred in the Rheinbund. Prussian major Ferdinand von Schill led an unsanctioned military rebellion, which ultimately failed. The most thorough account is Sam Mustafa's *The Long Ride of Major von Schill* (2008), which details the origin and course of the revolt, as well as the impact of the rebellion on German memory.

Following the victory over Austria, Napoleon did not return to the field until 1812. The Russian campaign stands at the crossroads of Napoleon's empire, from its pinnacle to its rapid decline. The English-language histories of the 1812 campaign have been drawn substantially from French and French allied accounts. Russian sources are numerous, but Western scholars' inability to either read Russian or access the archives prohibited the use of such sources through the twentieth century and continues to cause problems after the end of the Cold War.

Perhaps the most widely available Russian source is the translation of Eugene Tarlé's *Napoleon's Invasion of Russia, 1812*

(1942). The date of its publication is quite revealing, as the German invasion of Russia during the Second World War made the Soviet Union, the United States, and Great Britain unlikely allies. Tarlé used available French and Russian sources to create one of the few histories of the war that included a substantial Russian account. Since the end of the Cold War, and the opening of Russian archives, quite a number of excellent studies have appeared.

Among the scholars that dedicated their research to the Russian perspective of 1812 are Dominic Lieven and Alexander Mikaberidze. Lieven's *Russia against Napoleon* (2010) is not solely concerned with 1812, but more than half the book focuses on that campaign. The history is written through Russian eyes, and the research is outstanding. Lieven's history is the foremost account of Russia during the Napoleonic Wars. Alexander Mikaberidze has done more than any other Napoleonic scholar to make Russian documents accessible to the non-Russian-reading historical world through his translations of documents, memoirs, and diaries. In terms of 1812, Mikaberidze wrote two highly detailed accounts of the battles of Borodino, *The Battle of Borodino: Napoleon Against Kutuzov* (2007), and the Berezina, *The Battle of the Berezina: Napoleon's Great Escape* (2010). His knowledge of Napoleonic historiography, and understanding of the strategy, operations, and tactics, makes Mikaberidze's works invaluable. Lieven and Mikaberidze must be consulted in any research on 1812 before or after reviewing the standard campaign literature.

There are so many histories on 1812 that a discussion of some of the best primary and secondary sources would be most helpful. The two classic firsthand accounts of the campaign through French eyes are Armand-Augustin-Louis de Caulaincourt, *With Napoleon in Russia* (1935), and Philippe de Ségur, *Napoleon's Russian Campaign* (1958). Both men served as officers on Napoleon's staff during the invasion. Caulaincourt accompanied Napoleon during his two-week journey from Vilna to Paris in December 1812. Their memoirs are generally reliable. For sources from the soldier's perspective Adrien Jean Baptiste François Bourgogne, *The Memoirs of Sergeant Bourgogne* (1979), and Jakob Walter, *The Diary of a Napoleonic Foot Soldier* (1991), are accessible and provide insight into the campaign from the perspectives of a noncommissioned officer in the French Imperial Guard and a soldier in the Württemberg contingent.[1]

In recent years Russian primary sources have been translated, and are available to the English reader. Two titles of particular interest are Alexis Ermolov, *The Czar's General* (2005), edited and translated by Mikaberidze, and Denis Davydov, *In the Service of the Tsar against Napoleon* (2006), edited and translated by Gregory Troubetzkoy. Davydov commanded cavalry in 1812, leading successful partisan operations against the French. Ermelov (also spelled Yermelov) served at Borodino and throughout the war. He played a significant role in the arguments among the Russian high command concerning the best approach to dealing with Napoleon. To that end, Alexander Mikaberidze's article, "The Conflict of Command in the Russian Army in 1812" (2002), is important in understanding the infighting that occurred among the Russian military leadership.

Some of the best general histories of the campaign provide balanced and accessible analysis. Among those recommended

---

1   There are multiple English editions of Caulaincourt, de Ségur, and Bourgogne.

are Curtis Cate, *The War of Two Emperors* (1985), Richard K. Riehn, *1812: Napoleon's Russian Campaign* (1990), Christopher Duffy, *Borodino and the War of 1812* (1972), Paul Britten Austin, *1812: Napoleon's Invasion of Russia* (2000), and Adam Zamoyski, *Moscow 1812: Napoleon's Fatal March* (2004). Carl von Clausewitz, *The Campaign of 1812 in Russia* (1843, reprinted in 1992), is a solid primary source from the venerable Prussian general serving on Czar Alexander's staff.

There are several key works on the impact of the retreat from Moscow. Mikaberidze's book *The Battle of the Berezina* (2010) is highly recommended. Paul Britten Austin's *1812: The Great Retreat* (1996) comprises primary accounts. Lastly, Frederick C. Schneid, "The Dynamics of Defeat: French Army Leadership, December 1812–March 1813" (1999), examines the effect of the defeat on the morale of the marshals and generals of the French Imperial Army.

The debacle in Russia led to a rather rapid collapse of Napoleon's empire. Less than eighteen months after the defeat in Russia, Napoleon went into exile. The military history of the 1813 campaign was initially accessible through Petre's 1813 and 1814 histories, but in the past decade there have been several good books and articles on the end of the empire in central Europe. The best and most recent are Michael V. Leggiere, *Napoleon and Berlin* (2002) and *The Fall of Napoleon* (2007). Leggiere offers readers a decidedly Prussian view of the campaign. His first book examines the reconstruction of the Prussian army after 1812 and the successful defense of Berlin against two determined French offensives. Leggiere's latter book is the first of a two-volume study of the allied invasion of France. Volume one is concerned with the diplomatic and military preparations for operations after the coalition victory at Leipzig in October 1813. The first third of the book addresses allied arguments and movements in Germany at the end of 1813. In both volumes Leggiere has culled the Prussian military archives and provides a detailed account of operations.

The secret to allied victory in 1813 rested more with the nature of the coalition rather than French weakness. The success of the Sixth Coalition is critical to understanding Napoleon's ultimate defeat. Leggiere does a wonderful job in both books, thereby superseding the classic article by Gordon Craig, "Problems of Coalition Warfare: The Military Alliance against Napoleon, 1813–1814"(1966). Philip Dwyer contributed to the recent exploration of coalition victory in "Self-Interest versus the Common Cause: Austria, Prussia and Russia against Napoleon" (2008). Dominic Lieven, *Russia Against Napoleon*, contributed the second half of the post-1812 narrative to the war in 1813–1814. Finally, Jonathon Riley attempted to tie the Napoleonic Wars and the War of 1812 in North America together in an ambitious work, *Napoleon and the World War of 1813* (2000). Jeremy Black did the same in *The War of 1812 in the Age of Napoleon* (2009), but looked at the war in North America from London's perspective and the difficulty of managing conflicts in two hemispheres.

The coalition war against France did not fare well in the spring 1813, but Austria's participation after August 1813 turned the tide. Rothenberg, *Napoleon's Great Adversary* (1982), contributed a chapter on the Austrian army and war effort, but Leggiere and Llewellyn Cook have since expanded significantly on the subject. Llewellyn Cook produced an invaluable dissertation on Karl Philipp, Prince of Schwarzenberg and the

Austrian army, and while that work has not yet been published, Cook has also published several articles on Schwarzenberg in the *Selected Papers of the Consortium on the Revolutionary Era* (1994, 1995, and 2008). Leggiere capitalized on Cook's work and developed it further in his last book, *The Fall of Napoleon*, and in his "Austrian Grand Strategy and the Invasion of France in 1814" (2007).

Napoleon's defeat in 1814 and first exile led to a ten-month hiatus from war. Upon his return to France in 1815, the coalition reformed and the Campaign of the Hundred Days, also know as the Waterloo Campaign, commenced. There are an incredible number of books on the Battle of Waterloo. Virtually all examine the campaign in Belgium from the French and British perspective. The classic work is Henry Houssaye, *1815, Waterloo* (English translation 1900). The role of the Prussians in many of these accounts is supplemental to the strategy of Arthur Wellesley, the 1st Duke of Wellington. The historiography of the campaign falls largely into the traditional realm, with little focus on the ancillary fronts on the Rhine, Alps, and Pyrenees. To this end, there is a lacuna in the literature. A history encompassing all of the fronts is desperately needed, as it would essentially end any question of whether the Battle of Waterloo mattered. Histories of the battle have focused squarely on the events of June 18 and the mistakes made, either on the field or the failure of Marshal Emmanuel de Grouchy to properly pursue the Prussian army after the French victory at Ligny. Regardless, a comprehensive history of the Hundred Days would make it abundantly clear that Napoleon lacked the resources to wage a successful war against the coalition, even if he had won at Waterloo.

Placing historical events in the larger context of European and world developments is the specialty of Jeremy Black. His book, *The Battle of Waterloo* (2010), attempts to do the same by exploring the grand strategy, tactical theory, and technological developments. Some years earlier Italian journalist Alessandro Barbero's *The Battle: A New History of Waterloo* (2006) provided another account, placing the Prussians squarely in the course of events. What has changed from the traditional narratives to these new histories is the increasing presence of the Prussian army. The Waterloo Campaign is notable for the cooperation of the Anglo-Allied Army under the Duke of Wellington and the Prussian Army under Field Marshal Gebhard Leberecht von Blücher. Napoleon conducted a strategically insightful offensive to keep their armies apart, and after defeating the Prussians at Ligny he moved to isolate and destroy Wellington at Waterloo. Unfortunately for Napoleon, Blücher rallied his army and arrived on Napoleon's flank on June 18.

The Prussians played a significant role in the historiography of the Hundred Days. British military historian Capt. William Siborne caused controversy in the 1840s when he published *History of the Waterloo Campaign* (1844, reprinted in 1990). His account found disfavor with the Duke of Wellington and his adherents, and Siborne spent many years under a cloud. Part of the issue was his perspective on the cooperation between Wellington and Blücher, and the extent to which the Prussians played the seminal role in saving Wellington from defeat. Siborne's current champion is independent historian Peter Hofschroer. In his *1815, the Waterloo Campaign: Wellington, His German Allies and the Battles of Ligny and Quatre Bras* (2006) and subsequent books on Wellington and the Hundred Days,

Hofschroer single-handedly attempts to challenge Wellington's accounts of the campaign and establish Waterloo as a "Germanic victory." This phrase is too loaded and purposefully contentious; nonetheless, Hofschroer's histories have compelled Napoleonic historians to reexamine the traditional Anglo-narratives.

The Battle of Waterloo was the culmination of a campaign lasting less than a week and involving four battles. The French won three of the four, but the fourth was the most important. The Battle of Ligny on June 16, 1815, was hard fought and led to the collapse of the Prussian army—albeit temporarily. Several historians have produced accessible books on the subject, including Andrew Uffindel, *The Eagle's Last Triumph: Napoleon's Victory at Ligny, June 1815* (2006). Although the world does not need another book on the Battle of Waterloo, an archival study of the Battle of Ligny would be most welcome.

In all, the campaigns of the Napoleonic Wars have received considerable attention, but there is room for archival-based histories and historical narratives from the Prussian, Russian, and Austrian perspectives. Historians such as Alexander Mikaberidze and Michael Leggiere are making progress in this area, but there is more to do. Strategic and operational histories have fallen out of fashion when based on the same printed primary sources. Archival histories that are eminently readable, and analytical, would strengthen the field and widen the availability of scholarly literature.

4

SATELLITES AND MINOR STATES: PUPPETS OR INDEPENDENT ACTORS?

Perhaps one of the least researched and most important aspects of the Napoleonic Wars is the satellite, clients, and allied states of Napoleon's empire. They represented virtually all the minor powers of Europe, including two new kingdoms created by Napoleon and the Grand Duchy of Warsaw, a reduced Polish state. The respective armies of these states constituted a significant portion of Napoleon's military power after 1807. Satellite and allied armies made up 30 percent of his strength in central Europe in 1809, and throughout the Peninsular War. During the invasion of Russia in 1812, more than 50 percent of his Grande Armée included non-French troops. The reason for the lack of historical emphasis on Napoleon's "foreign" armies can be found in the traditional perspective of the Napoleonic Wars as a conflict fought between Napoleon and the major European powers. There was little room in the historiography prior to 1990 and the end of the Cold War to examine the role of "minor powers." It was believed that they lacked the ability to conduct policies independent of the major powers and were essentially pawns in a chess game played by Napoleon, Prince Klemens von Metternich, Tsar Alexander I, and others. More recent histories have challenged the prevailing narrative, arguing that the princes of these states approached the rival powers of Europe in a similar fashion as their predecessors had in the past.

The first and most important book in English on the satellites is Owen Connelly, *Napoleon's Satellite Kingdoms* (1965). Connelly's book is a military and institutional history of the satellite kingdoms and their armies. He is only concerned with those states created or ruled by Napoleon's family members, the kingdoms of Italy, Naples, Holland, Westphalia, and Spain. These kingdoms formed the anchor states of the Grand Empire. Although Spain was far more a liability than asset, the other kingdoms provided valuable manpower and resources for the French imperial armies. Napoleon integrated these armies into his military system. Instead of deploying them as independent entities, he divided them among the regional French imperial armies. John Elting, *Swords Around A Throne: Napoleon's Grande Armée* (1988), provides a detailed examination of Napoleon's army but dedicates only a single chapter to the satellite and allied armies. Elting acknowledges the significant role played by these forces but is more interested in their organization and role within the larger imperial military machine.

Of the satellite kingdoms, the army of the Kingdom of Italy has been studied the most in the past twenty years. These histories focus on two primary questions:

1. To what extent did the Napoleonic kingdom influence the *Risorgimento*, the nineteenth-century movement for Italian unification?

2. What was the practical impact and reception of
    Napoleonic rule in Italy?

Franco Della Peruta was the first historian to address the
Italian army, but his book, *Esercito e società in Italia napoleonica*
(1988) has not been translated into English. A synopsis
appeared as a chapter, "War and Society in Napoleonic Italy:
the Armies of the Kingdom of Italy at Home and Abroad," in
Society and Politics in the Age of the Risorgimento (1991). Della
Peruta saw the Napoleonic experience as entirely negative, viewing the Napoleonic regime as inherently oppressive and the military experience as imperialistic. He approaches the subject
through a clearly Marxist lens, which provides a coherent model
for his application of history.

In his articles, Alexander Grab concurs with Della Peruta concerning the army of the Kingdom of Italy. Both "Army, State and
Society: Conscription and Desertion in Napoleonic Italy, 1802–
1814" (1995) in the *Journal of Modern History* and "State Power,
Brigandage and Rural Resistance in Napoleonic Italy" in *European
History Quarterly* (1995), examine the weight of Napoleonic conscription in the Italian kingdom and the response of the population to that policy. More recently Grab published a chapter,
"Conscription and Desertion in Napoleonic Italy, 1802–1814,"
in *Conscription in the Napoleonic Era* (2009) that repeats much
of his earlier work, but he has toned down his assault on the
Napoleonic regime. In all, both Grab and Della Peruta see Italians
as victims of the Napoleonic regime and its military policies.

The same year Grab published his articles on Napoleonic
Italy, Frederick C. Schneid published *Soldiers of Napoleon's
Kingdom of Italy: Army, State, and Society, 1800–1815* (1995).

The book is both an institutional and socio-military study. Schneid challenges Della Peruta and Grab's perspectives, arguing that the Napoleonic experience was vital to fostering Italian nationalism. Despite substantial antipathy for conscription policies, Schneid believes that the shared military experiences helped break down regional differences and animosity. More recently, Schneid contributed a succinct chapter on the "Army of the Kingdom of Italy" in *Armies of the Napoleonic Wars* (2011) that integrates some of the new work on this subject, drawn particularly from Virgilio Ilari et al.'s *Storia Militare del Regno Italico (1802–1814)* (2004). This three-volume history is the most thorough examination of the military history of the Kingdom of Italy. Unfortunately, it is not available in English.

The Italian experience included the creation of the Kingdom of Naples in 1806. There is very little, however, in English on the military history of the Kingdom of Naples. Milton Finley produced a fine history of its conquest and the ensuing guerrilla war, *The Most Monstrous of Wars: The Napoleonic Guerrilla War in Southern Italy, 1806–1811* (1994). Other books on this topic are in short supply. Frederick C. Schneid's *Napoleon's Italian Campaigns, 1805–1815* (2002) provides a narrative of the campaign of 1806 fought between the Franco-Italian army and the army of the Kingdom of the Two Sicilies. William Flayhart, *Counterpoint to Trafalgar: The Anglo-Russian Invasion of Naples, 1805–1806* (1992), provides an extremely useful account of the role of the Neapolitan kingdom, prior to its conquest and during the War of the Third Coalition. A much more detailed two-volume work appeared in 2005—Virgilio Ilari and Giancarlo Boeri, *Le Due Sicile nelle Guerre Napoleoniche (1800–1815)*—but it, too, is unavailable in English.

The material available on the Kingdom of Holland is sorely lacking. Simon Schama, *Patriots and Liberators: Revolution in the Netherlands, 1780–1813* (1992), is the best comprehensive work in English. Although not a military history, Schama provides extensive details on the fiscal and military policies of the Napoleonic kingdom. The Dutch revolutionaries allied early on with the Revolutionary French, only to lose their independence as a republic and be forged into an imperial kingdom under Napoleon's brother Louis. After 1810, Napoleon removed his brother and annexed the kingdom directly into Imperial France. Recently, Mark van Hattem and Mariska Pool, "Four Men and a Woman: Remarkable Dutch Experiences during the Russian Campaign of Napoleon in 1812" in *Selected Papers of the Consortium on the Revolutionary Era, 1750–1850* (2008), introduced a wonderful perspective of the Dutch military experience in 1812. They offer some primary source accounts of the Russian campaign from a non-French perspective. This chapter was a part of their larger work, *In the Wake of Napoleon: The Dutch in Time of War: 1792–1815* (2006). To that end Alexander Mikaberidze, *The Battle of the Berezina: Napoleon's Great Escape* (2010), provides extensive narrative of the role of the Dutch and German troops during the retreat from Moscow, and their critical role on the Berezina in November 1812.

The Kingdom of Westphalia, the only German satellite, has received new interest in the past decade. The kingdom was carved largely from Hanover and Hessen-Kassel. The military tradition of these German territories in the eighteenth century has been studied well, yet no examination of the army of the Kingdom of Westphalia appeared until several years ago. Michael Pavkovic, "Recruitment and Conscription in the Kingdom of

Westphalia: The Palladium of Westphalian Freedom" in *Conscription in the Napoleonic Era* (2009), provides a current overview of the military institution of the Napoleonic kingdom and places it in the context of the historical military traditions of its predecessor territories. Glenn Lamar's biography, *Jerome Bonaparte: The War Years, 1800–1815* (2000), provides a narrative of Westphalian military policy and operations under Napoleon's brother Jerome, King of Westphalia.

The examination of satellite kingdoms offers insight into only one aspect of the larger empire commanded by Napoleon. Practically every European state at one time or another was allied to France. Thus the study of minor powers in the Napoleonic Wars must look beyond those states dynastically tied to Napoleon. As with much of the history of Europe, the post–Cold War era permitted and influenced a new generation of historians that looked beyond the power-politics paradigm. Recent histories of eighteenth- and nineteenth-century Europe are introducing the idea that minor states were capable of making independent decisions and taking action based on the events of the day.

Peter H. Wilson's work on the "Third Germany," those parts of Germany other than Austria or Prussia, includes *German Armies: War and German Politics, 1648–1806* (1998) and provided a valuable foundation for future study of the policies and actions of the German princes outside the traditional Austro-Prussian interpretation of German history. His books address the situation in pre-Rheinbund Germany and offer insight into the constants of the German princely and military politics that played an essential role in the actions of the princes after the abolition of the Holy Roman Empire.

The armies of the Rheinbund princes contributed vital military resources to the French imperial armies. Jean Sauzey's six-volume history of the armies of the Confederation of the Rhine, *Les Allemandes sous les Aigles Française: Essai sur les Troupes de la Confédération du Rhin, 1806–1814*, 6 vols. (1902–1912), is considered the standard work on the topic of German military contributions to the Napoleonic Empire. The traditional perspective of German princes caught between Napoleonic France, Austria, and Prussia, however, has been rejected in recent scholarship. It is clear that the German princes, who had already sought to steer the course between Prussian and Austrian politics as early as 1792, did not wish to be drawn into a larger conflict. Indeed, Peter H. Wilson, "German Military Preparedness at the Eve of the Revolutionary Wars" in *Warfare in Europe, 1792–1815* (2007), challenges the traditional argument that German armies were ossified by absolutist principles and that their rigid military system was responsible for defeat. The importance of Wilson's work is in his willingness to explore the nature of German policies and institutions outside the traditional framework. By studying the individual princes and their policies, students of history can properly reject a simplistic bipolar (Prusso-Austrian) German polity, a process that can be equally applied to military policies. Gunther E. Rothenberg also published an essay, "A Massachusetts Yankee in Elector Karl Theodor's Court" (2008), on the Bavarian military reforms from 1787 to 1801, which laid the foundations for future reforms in the soon-to-be German kingdom.

Wilson's scholarship, thus far, stops with the abolition of the Holy Roman Empire in 1806 and its replacement with the Rheinbund. The anchor states of Westphalia, Bavaria,

Württemberg, Baden, and Saxony provided substantial manpower to Napoleon's armies. The study of the Rheinbund and its military contributions has benefited greatly from the work of John H. Gill, *With Eagles to Glory: Napoleon and His German Allies in the 1809 Campaign* (1992), which was the first major English publication on the subject. Gill took an institutional and operational approach to the critical contribution of German forces during the 1809 campaign against Austria. Gill succeeded in introducing a German narrative to a traditionally French-dominated history. His history, *1809: Thunder on the Danube: Napoleon's Defeat of the Habsburgs*, 3 vols. (2008–2010), further integrates the role of the Rheinbund armies into Napoleon's victory. It is one of the new histories of the Napoleonic Wars to take advantage of the availability of new sources on satellites and allies, as well as the willingness of the author to integrate them into a full account. Finally, Gill contributed a chapter on the Rheinbund troops in the Peninsular War, "Vermin, Scorpions, and Mosquitoes: The *Rheinbund* in the Peninsula," in Ian Fletcher, ed., *The Peninsular War* (1998). There is a great deal of fertile ground here for future historians, as German histories on the military institutions of these regimes are scarce in any language.

The Grand Duchy of Warsaw remains a rather obscure state within Napoleon's empire. Polish military contributions exceeded all other satellite and allied states, but the Grand Duchy, created in 1808, was not an independent entity ruled by a relative of the French emperor. Frederick Augustus I, King of Saxony, was made Grand Duke of Warsaw by Napoleon in 1808. The purposeful union of these states had historical precedence in the eighteenth century, but the Saxon king governed from Dresden and had a rather laissez-faire attitude toward Polish politics. Despite the considerable strategic position of Poland, and its military contributions, it is the least studied of the satellite states. The most recent academic discussion is Jarosław Czubaty's brief "Army of the Duchy of Warsaw" in *Armies of the Napoleonic Wars* (2011), but a detailed study in English is long overdue.

The historical narrative placed the satellite and client states of the Grand Empire in the larger debate concerning Napoleonic occupation policy and whether the Grand Empire was created by accident or design. To this end, the general historiography interprets the development of the empire as accident. Its creation was not preplanned by grand design but was developed over the course of larger events and shaped by the conclusion of individual campaigns. Certainly, there is no clear evidence that Napoleon possessed a pre-conceived notion of the specific shape of his grand empire. His general desire to expand the borders of France to their "natural frontiers" is perhaps the most one can say for certain. From this perspective, the role of minor powers was completely subject to the interests of major powers. This fits well into the traditional narrative of Napoleonic history. A more careful study, however, seems to indicate that in Europe post-1763, the ability of major powers to use and abuse the minor states became less certain than it had been in the past. Schneid, "Kings, Clients and Satellites in the Napoleonic Imperium" (2008), argues that the creation and maintenance of the Grand Empire was based on historic French relationships, and the respective minor powers saw advantage in allying with Napoleon.

It is clear that any realignment of minor powers elicited significant response from the major powers. Thus, when the Austrian emperor Joseph II attempted to trade Belgium for

Bavaria twice in the 1770s and 1780s, armies mobilized. During the Revolutionary Wars, French treaties with Prussia and later Austria included specific agreements concerning the fate of Italian and German territories. Venice lost its independence after centuries to Austrian occupation in 1797, and the German princes on the west bank of the Rhine were cast out after French annexation in 1794. During the first years of the Consulate the Holy Roman Empire underwent significant administrative and territorial reforms in the Imperial Recess of 1803. The German princes sought French and Russian support for their own designs, in conjunction with the major powers. The transformation of Germany in 1803 did not mark the death knell of the empire, according to Peter Wilson, "Bolstering the Prestige of the Habsburgs: The End of the Holy Roman Empire in 1806" (2006), but was an attempt by German princes to establish some sense of greater independence from the Reich.

The relationship between Bavaria, Baden, Nassau, and Saxony improved during the years of peace between 1802 and 1805. As war loomed, the French, Austrians, and Russians, who sought allies, approached them. Ultimately, the determination to ally with France in 1805 was not made out of duress but after careful, albeit risky, decision making. The response of minor states to the War of the Third Coalition is explored in detail in Schneid, *Napoleon's Conquest of Europe: The War of the Third Coalition* (2005). Subsequently, the military role of the Rheinbund during the collapse of the Napoleonic Empire has only been addressed tangentially. The most detailed examination in English is Daniel Klang, "Bavaria and the War of Liberation" (1965). Recently, Michael V. Leggiere, *Napoleon and Berlin* and *The Fall of Napoleon* (2002 and 2007), has placed the fate of the Rheinbund princes, particularly Saxony and Bavaria, in the context of the 1813 campaign and coalition strategy after Leipzig.

Napoleon may have established a coherent imperial system throughout Europe, but his enemies also employed minor states in their alliance systems. Sweden, the Ottoman Empire, and Portugal all participated in the wars. The Ottoman Empire first fought against, and then with the French through 1812. Virginia Aksan's *Ottoman Wars 1700–1870* (2007) is the best general history of the Ottoman Empire's role during the period from Selim III to Mustapha IV. In terms of Sweden's role, Christer Jörgensen, *The Anglo-Swedish Alliance against Napoleonic France* (2004), is quite good. Fredrik Thisner also produced a chapter on conscription in Sweden in Stoker, Schneid, and Blanton's *Conscription in the Napoleonic Era* (2009).

For too long the role of minor European states was subordinated to the actions and interests of the major powers. Clearly, France, Austria, Prussia, Russia, and Great Britain possessed the military and economic power to ply, cajole, and threaten minor states. They had traditionally seen these states as a source of military and economic support. The recent military histories of the eighteenth-century wars make it apparent that Britain and Austria desperately needed external sources of military power to project their influence effectively in central Europe. Britain is a primary case, as much of its military power in the eighteenth century came in the form of hired German regiments. Napoleon's domination of Central Europe forced the powers to either draw on their own meager resources, or find new ones. The role of minor states in the Napoleonic Wars is fertile ground for further research.

The minor powers possessed their own history, independent of the interests of the France, Austria, Prussia, Russia, and Great Britain. These histories intersect at several levels with the major powers. This is particularly true in regard to power politics but equally applicable to domestic developments. The implication of this relationship is that popular unrest in Europe during the French Revolution and Napoleonic Era has recently caught the attention of Napoleonic historians. The insurrection in Calabria, the Tyrol, and Germany are already understood in the context of the wars, and the Spanish guerrillas have an entirely independent body of literature. Charles Esdaile, editor of *Popular Resistance in the French Wars* (2005), and Michael Broers, *Napoleon's Other War* (2010), joined the discourse. This direction is part of the weight and impact of social and cultural history, so dominant in academia. These histories provide some insight into the military implications of the popular resistance but are almost exclusively focused on the cause: Napoleonic policy. More studies are—no doubt—in progress, but, as with the history of the revolt in the Vendée during the French Revolution, there is a need to place the rebellions in the context of regional and national history, integrating them within the military history of the era.

ARMIES OF THE NAPOLEONIC WARS

The dominance of French and British sources in the narrative of the Napoleonic Wars has left a significant imbalance in the historiography of Napoleonic armies. It is quite easy to be overwhelmed with books and articles on the composition, structure, organization, and nature of the French Imperial Army. Similarly, the work on the British army is rather easy to find. The cause of the problem was not isolated to a lack of English-language sources, but also due to the tendency of historians in Europe to neglect the armies of the major powers to the same extent as they did the armies of the satellites and minor powers. In the past twenty years an increasing number of histories focusing on Napoleon's enemies have appeared. In addition to the study of military institutions and organization, conscription policy and the social composition of armies have become significant focuses in the past two decades.

The French Imperial Army was the most experienced and best led in Europe in 1805. At least half of all soldiers in 1803 served in one campaign during the French Revolution. The officer corps, too, comprised long-standing veterans. Historians uniformly agree that Napoleon was not an originator but an innovator in terms of military reforms. Gunther Rothenberg, *The Art of Warfare in the Age of Napoleon* (1976), provides the standard overview of the institutionalization of the corps system, general staff (*Grande Quartier Generale*), and separation of military branches (infantry, cavalry, and artillery). A more detailed study is Col. John R. Elting (Ret.), *Swords Around a Throne: Napoleon's Grande Armée* (1988).

Elting was one of the foremost historians of the Napoleonic Wars and a coauthor of the classic *Military History and Atlas of the Napoleonic Wars* (1965), which is part of the West Point Military History Series. *Swords Around a Throne* dissects Napoleon's army into its component parts including chapters on the engineering corps, medical personnel, penal battalions, logistical officers, and vivandières. The latter were the female camp followers who provided supplies and a variety of services to the soldiers on the campaign. Thomas Cardoza, a former student of Rothenberg, published an excellent history of this semi-official military institution, *Intrepid Women: Cantinières and Vivandières of the French Army* (2010). Elting utilized many of the standard French sources on the imperial army and provides a lucid and meticulous history of Napoleon's army. The beginner in Napoleonic history can also access Georges Blond's classic, *La Grande Armée*, which was translated into English in 1995. Blond takes a narrative approach to the history of the French Imperial Army from 1805 to 1815.

How Napoleon fed his army is very much part of understanding military strategy and operations. Certainly, the perception that Napoleon's army "marched on its stomach" has persisted in many accounts. Peter Wetzler, *War and Subsistence: The Sambre and Meuse Army in 1794* (1985), made the first exploration of logistics in the French revolutionary armies. His book remains important but underutilized. In regard to the imperial army, Martin van Creveld, *Supplying War: Logistics from Wallenstein to Patton* (1979), made the first English-language analysis concerning 1805, when Napoleon rapidly moved his army from the Channel Coast to Germany. Frederick C. Schneid, *Napoleon's Conquest of Europe* (2005), rejected the traditional view of Napoleonic logistics in 1805, arguing that Napoleon relied on his German allies to supply his forces during their march on Ulm. Logistical studies recently benefited from the award-winning article by John Morgan, "War Feeding War? The Impact of Logistics upon the Occupation of Catalonia" (2009). The field is still in its infancy, and much more needs to be done.

The ability to feed ever-expanding imperial armies required greater organization and institutional capacity. Everett Dague ably handled the military administration of the First Empire in *Napoleon and the First Empire's Ministries of War and Military Administration* (2006). His book should be read in conjunction with Howard Brown's 1995 work on the French military bureaucracy, *War, Revolution and the Bureaucratic State*.

Most of the general histories of the Napoleonic Wars provide extensive discussions on the structure and composition of the French army during the respective campaigns. The study of conscription policy became a central part of the historiography during the1980s. The Vietnam War had a profound effect on historians, and the field of military history was no exception. The draft in the United States and the reaction against the war laid the foundations for the production of numerous studies concerning Napoleonic conscription policy in the decades that followed. The overwhelming majority of conscription histories portray it as an oppressive institution that fed Napoleon's armies. It was clearly the most unpopular aspect of the Napoleonic regime.

The Jourdan Law of 1798 established conscription as an institution in Revolutionary France. The voluntary levies that fed French armies from 1791 through 1792, followed by the famed and often overblown levée en masse of 1793, provided ample troops for a state at war with much of Europe. By 1796, however, the ranks of French armies had been depleted through desertion, attrition, and casualties. The conclusion of the war of the First Coalition ended the immediate military threat, but anticipation of a new war led the Directory, the revolutionary government du jour, to establish a reliable system to maintain the strength of the army. The Jourdan Law became the legal basis for Napoleonic conscription.

According to data provided by André Corvisier in *Histoire militaire de la France* (1992), French armies averaged 380,000 men during the Revolution. The years 1793–1794, when the levée en masse raised the army to 750,000 men, are the exception. During the Napoleonic Wars, the French army averaged 500,000 men. This number includes conscription from the imperial departments of France, those in Belgium, and the west bank of the Rhine and Italy. France annexed these regions after 1794 and formerly recognized by agreement after 1797–1801.[1]

---

1   Recognition of the annexation of Belgium and the west bank of the Rhine was a fundamental part of the Peace of Campo Formio (1797) and later reaffirmed in the Treaty of Lunéville (1801). The annexation of Piedmont in 1802 violated Lunéville but was done nonetheless.

Isser Woloch made the first significant foray into conscription policy with "Napoleonic Conscription: State Power and Civil Society" (1986). His exploratory article set the stage for his larger work, *The New Regime* (1994), which included a solid chapter on conscription in Napoleonic France. He argued that conscription, despite its lack of popularity, was the most successful policy instituted by the Napoleonic administration. Alan Forrest published what remains the authoritative work on the subject, *Conscripts and Deserters: The French Army and Society during the Revolution and Empire* (1989). Much of Forrest's book is concerned with the impact of conscription on French society. To that end he provides ample research on the conscription process, but the majority of his book examines the reaction to conscription. Popular response to Napoleonic conscription policy was manifest in desertion and *insoumission*, the failure of recruits to appear at the assigned regimental depots. According to Forrest, desertion and insoumission reflected an active resistance to the Napoleonic regime.

One of the dilemmas for historians is the imbalance in the exploration of conscription and desertion from the Revolution to the Napoleonic Era. By placing the revolutionary levies and the levée en masse in the same context as Napoleonic conscription, it is unmistakable that soldiers in the revolutionary armies deserted at greater rates than during the Napoleonic Era. If the levée en masse raised the strength of the French army to 750,000 in late 1793, then what explains the drop to 380,000 in 1796? Forrest and other historians concede significant desertion during the Revolution but prefer to spend more time on desertion as resistance to the Napoleonic regime. What is needed is a proper examination of conscription from its ad hoc voluntary levies of 1791–1793 to the formal institutionalization in 1797 and thereafter. This would permit historians to place desertion and resistance to conscription in its proper context.

The decided focus on conscription as an oppressive Napoleonic policy also warped the understanding of the institution in relation to the development of the power of the centralized state, and the ability to mobilize, train, and equip large numbers of the male population without negatively affecting the national and, more importantly, local economies. Indeed, much of the history of conscription makes the argument that the peasantry was drafted at far greater rates than were members of the middle class and nobility. Further, the ability of individuals to purchase substitutes—a practice ended in 1810—is given as evidence of social imbalance of conscription. The problem with this argument is that as a primarily agricultural society, the peasantry represented more than 70 percent of the population. Logic and statistics dictate that the peasantry would therefore always be proportionally represented in the army.

Macro-histories of conscription have been the standard, but recently micro-histories have begun to appear. Hassan Ben Toutouh, "Resistance to Conscription and Local Conflicts in the Department of the Dyle (1801–1806)" (2008), is a fascinating examination of the impact of conscription policy in the Belgian departments of Imperial France. Ben Toutouh explains that the response to conscription was far more complex than historians have allowed. Desertion, too, was viewed as problematic to the local population because it meant others had to bear the burden of replacing the deserter from the community, or in adjacent towns.

The authors in Donald Stoker, Frederick C. Schneid, and Harold Blanton, eds., *Conscription in the Napoleonic Era: A*

Revolution in Military Affairs? (2009), argued that conscription was revolutionary in its French iteration, but the respective allies and enemies of France only applied those elements of conscription policy that would not disturb the social and political order at home. To that end, Napoleonic conscription policy concluded with the restoration of the Bourbon monarchy in 1815. In 1818, according to Thomas Hippler, *Citizens, Soldiers and National Armies: Military Service in France and Germany, 1789–1830* (2008), after heated debate, the Chamber of Deputies restored a modified conscription system. It was not until the Third French Republic in 1873 that universal conscription returned to France.

The enormous reliance on conscription to inflate Napoleon's army leads to the question of how he managed to maintain a highly effective system and motivate his soldiers. Alan Forrest, *Napoleon's Men: The Soldiers of the Revolution and Empire* (2002), uses letters from French soldiers to assess their perceptions of military service and the impact of the revolutionary levies and Napoleonic conscription on the individual. The examination of French military culture is the focus of the book by Michael Hughes, *Forging Napoleon's Grande Armée: Motivation, Military Culture, and Masculinity in the French Army* (2012).

Beyond the discussion of military organization, conscription, and the conduct of operations, the history of Napoleon's armies includes a number of biographies of marshals. An abundance of such works are available in French, but a sufficient number exist in English. An invaluable history of the marshalate remains David Chandler, ed., *Napoleon's Marshals* (1987). This history examines the twenty-six marshals of the empire with specific attention to their military biographies. The chapters were written by long-standing military historians such as Peter Young, Donald Horward, Gunther Rothenberg, Charles Esdaile, and John Elting, among others. One of the most important biographies is John G. Gallaher, *The Iron Marshal* (1976), a study of the life of Marshal Louis-Nicholas Davout. Gallaher also published biographies of two Napoleonic generals: *Dominique Vandamme: Napoleon's Enfant Terrible* (2008) and *General Alexandre Dumas* (1997), the father of the famous French novelist.

There are a number of biographies of Marshal Michel Ney, the "bravest of the brave." The standard biography is Raymond Horricks, *Marshal Ney: The Real and the Romance* (1982). A reprint of A. H. Atteridge, *Marshal Ney: The Bravest of the Brave* (1913, 2005), is also now available. In recent years Wayne Hanley, "Ney and Quatre Bras: An Invitation for Reevaluation" (2007) and "Between Sylla and Charybdis: Marshal Ney at Lons-le-Saulnier" (2008), has published articles analyzing Ney's military performance in 1815, challenging traditional interpretations. It is curious, however, that biographies of Marshal André Masséna or Alexandre Berthier, Napoleon's chief of staff, are not available in English.[2] Carola Oman's study of Eugène de Beauharnais, *Napoleon's Viceroy* (1966), remains an excellent source for the emperor's stepson and commander of the Army of Italy. There are no analytical studies of the Napoleonic officer corps except for Jean-Paul Bertaud's highly focused "Napoleon's Officers" (1986), but a broader examination of the entire officer corps is needed, dating back to the Revolution. Howard Brown's informative article "Politics, Professionalism, and the Fate of the

---

2   J. H. Marshall-Cornwall wrote the only English-language biography of Marshal André Masséna, *Marshal Masséna* (Oxford: Oxford University Press, 1965).

Army Generals after Thermidor" (1995) is a good start, followed by Rafe Blaufarb, *The French Army, 1750–1820: Careers, Talent, Merit* (2002).

The study of Napoleon's armies and his lieutenants are only half the story. Any student or scholar pursuing this period must also be familiar with coalition armies. Failure to address the military institutions and leadership of the rest of Europe will produce a monolithic history in which the opponents of the French emperor have no will of their own and simply fall prey to Napoleon's "genius." To that end, the study of European armies has never been easier in the post–Cold War era. Archives, multilateral perspectives, and secondary histories make research on these armies much easier.

Austria contributed more than any other continental power to the coalitions against Revolutionary and Napoleonic France. There is not, however, a great deal written in English on the Austrian army during the Revolutionary and Napoleonic Era. The seminal source is Gunther E. Rothenberg's *Napoleon's Great Adversary* (1982), as well as his later article "Shield of the Dynasty: Reflections on the Habsburg Army, 1649–1918" (2001). To Rothenberg, the Austrian army was a central pillar of the Habsburg dynasty. The composition, structure, leadership, strategy, and operations were developed and maintained in order to preserve the dynasty. This is the traditional view, and all historians writing after Rothenberg accept his interpretation. Michael Hochedlinger, Austrian military historian and former archivist at the *Kriegsarchiv* in Vienna, has written a great deal about the Habsburg Army in the eighteenth century, but he ended his *Austria's Wars of Emergence* (2003) with the conclusion of the War of the First Coalition. Hochedlinger published a good essay on the Habsburg officer corps in the late eighteenth century, "Mars Ennobled" (1999), which explores the culture of the Austrian officer corps during the eighteenth century, but his conclusion is equally applicable to the Revolution and empire. In his essay "The Early Modern Cinderella," in the *Austrian History Yearbook* (2001), Hochedlinger argued that while institutional and narrative histories of the Habsburg Empire have been written, there is a desperate need for a deeper study of the soldiers of the army.

A social-political study of the Austrian army during the Revolutionary and Napoleonic Wars is needed. There are several very good accounts of the army in the nineteenth century, but they address the composition of the army post-1848. The ethnic and national heterogeneity led to studies of the army during this age of nationalism, but scholars have ignored this reality prior to 1848. Arthur Boerke, "Conscription in the Habsburg Empire to 1815" (2009), examined Habsburg conscription policy through the Napoleonic Wars, concluding that the fear of universal conscription on the French model prevented the implementation of the policy after the defeats of 1805 and 1809. This argument is consistent with previous work by Rothenberg, *The Art of Warfare in the Age of Napoleon* and *Napoleon's Great Adversary* (1976 and 1982), and Lee Eysturlid, *The Formative Influences, Theories, and Campaigns of the Archduke Carl of Austria* (1999). Eysturlid, a former student of Rothenberg, studied the formative influences of the Archduke Charles, the premier Austrian military leader. Charles was an enlightened rationalist and feared popular unrest. He opposed conscription and support for the insurrection in the Tyrol in 1809, though it was declared in the name of the dynasty. The notion of universal conscription received assistance from the Archduke John, younger brother of

Charles and Kaiser Franz I. Regardless, the fear of nationalism and popular armies threatened the very fiber that held the dynasty together.

The Habsburg army after 1805 experienced a change in leadership and organization. The humiliating defeats at Ulm and Austerlitz secured the position of the Archduke Charles, brother of the Austrian emperor, as Generalissimus of the Habsburg army and president of the *Hofkriegsrat*, the Imperial War Council. John Gill, *1809: Thunder on the Danube*, 3 vols. (2008–2010), provides extensive details on the military reforms conducted by the archduke and adds a further layer to Rothenberg's exploration of the changes and tensions with the stalwarts at the Habsburg court. Charles's failure in 1809 led to his dismissal and the rise of Prince Karl zu Schwarzenberg. The prince commanded the Habsburg army from 1810 to 1815, and while he appeared to eliminate some of Charles's more controversial reforms, he successfully rebuilt and maintained the integrity of the army through the Russian campaign and the War of the Sixth Coalition. There are few sources dedicated to Schwarzenberg and the Habsburg army after Charles other than Rothenberg. Llew Cook, "Command in Crisis: The Army of Bohemia, May–August 1813" (2008), and Michael Leggiere, "Austrian Grand Strategy and the Invasion of France in 1814" (2007), provided a more detailed narrative and analysis. Leggiere's forthcoming second volume on 1814 will have much-needed new material.

For Russia's role, the dearth of English-language sources is rather disturbing. The Cold War severely restricted access of Western historians to the archives; only the memoirs and printed sources from the nineteenth century were available. F. Loraine

Petre consulted these printed sources in his books on 1807 and 1813, as he wrote prior to the First World War, but as mentioned in the previous chapter, only recently have historians been able to produce fine histories of the Russian army. Christopher Duffy, *Eagles over the Alps: Suvarov in Italy and Switzerland, 1799* (1998, reprinted in 1999), was the first significant book on the Russian army during the War of the Second Coalition. Duffy, however, is not a Russian historian, and only in the past decade have books by Russian specialists appeared. Janet M. Hartley, *Russia, 1762–1825: Military Power, the State, and the People* (2008), is highly detailed and documents history of Russia and its army from the reign of Catherine the Great to Alexander I. She challenged the notion of Russia as an eighteenth-century static military state. Russian military and foreign policy, Hartley argued, was a success by 1815, and after 1812, "Russia became the undisputed leading military power in Europe."[3] Although Habsburg historians may take issue with this statement, the majority of Hartley's research was conducted in the Russian state archives. To this end, Alexander Mikaberidze made substantial contributions to our understanding of the Russian army and its officers in the Napoleonic Wars in *The Russian Officer Corps in the Revolutionary and Napoleonic Wars, 1792–1815* (2005).

The composition of the Russian army has received some attention from Hartley, but most of the historical literature tends to take a broad sweeping approach. To that end, John L. Keep, *Soldiers of the Tsar: Army and Society in Russia, 1462–1874* (1985), and Elise Kimerling Wirtschafter, *From Serf to Russian Soldier* (1990), are recommended. These books provide general

3   Janet M. Hartley, *Russia, 1762–1825: Military Power, the State, and the People* (Westport, CT: Praeger, 2008), 3.

context to the Russian army, but they do not address the organization and institutions. The Russian army was the first of the coalition members to substantially overhaul its organizational structure after the defeat in 1807. The Russian army that faced Napoleon in 1812 was much more flexible, and rather similar to the French organizational structure. Unlike Austria, where Charles's reforms faced resistance, it appears that Russian military reforms were generally accepted. Conscription was not new to Russia, and the military obligation of recruits to serve for twenty-five years removed them from their respective villages and societies. Janet Hartley establishes that the lengthy duration of military service, and the fatalistic acceptance of the population to the loss of these individuals from the community, made conscription a rather politically safe and reliable institution. Mikaberidze provided the specific institutional process during the Napoleonic Wars in "Conscription in Russia" (2009). The centrality of Russia to the coalitions, and more specifically to the defeat of Napoleon in 1812, necessitates an extensive and detailed study of the Russian army during the Napoleonic Wars.

The Prussian army has received increasing attention in the past two decades. Although historians can find ample material on the Prussian army prior to the French Revolution, and during the Wars of German Unification, the number of histories on the French Revolutionary and Napoleonic Era remains thin. The earliest English-language work was William Shanahan, *Prussian Military Reform, 1786–1813* (1945). The interpretive and analytical structure of the book is typical of histories of the Prussian army during the Napoleonic Era with the focus on the origins and course of reforms before and after the debacle of 1806. Thus, Peter Paret, *Yorck and the Era of the Prussian Reform,*

1807–1815 (1966), and Charles White, *The Enlightened Soldier: Scharnhorst and the Militärische Gesellschaft in Berlin, 1801–1805* (1989), are excellent books but only if seeking information on the post–Jena-Auerstädt army. These histories are well researched and documented. They make it clear that the Prussian army through 1806 and thereafter was not an intellectually and militarily static institution, but one that kept in pace with European military thought and did not seek to rest on its laurels. The defeat of 1806, therefore, cleared the way for these reforms that existed in writing and discussions to be implemented. The dynamic presented is similar to the French military reforms before and after 1789.

The Prussian army was quite active from the death of Frederick the Great in 1786 through the French Revolutionary Wars. Historians have overlooked its military performance, as Prussia withdrew from the First Coalition in 1795 and did not return to the battlefield until 1806. Dennis Showalter, "Hubertusberg to Auerstädt: The Prussian Army in Decline?" and "Reform and Stability: Prussia's Military Dialectic from Hubertusberg to Waterloo" (1994 and 2012), argued that the Prussia's military performance prior to 1806 gave no indication of a decaying institution that would suffer ignominious defeat on the battlefield. Furthermore, he stressed that the Prussian army performed admirably in 1806 but was outgeneraled and outfought.

The most recent studies of the Prussian army during the Sixth Coalition are Michael V. Leggiere's books (2002 and 2007). Unlike with his predecessors, Leggiere's histories, particularly those sections directly addressing the Prussian army, are drawn from the German military archives. Leggiere is the leading historian on the Prussian army of the Napoleonic Wars and is currently writing a biography of its legendary commander, Field Marshal Gebhard von Blücher. Leggiere has also published numerous articles on the Prussian *Landwehr*, in simple terms a militia which included members of the middle class and those not of prime conscription age. He has added to an initial exploration by Dennis Showalter, "The Prussian Landwehr and Its Critics" (1971), almost four decades earlier. The reconstruction of the Prussian army in 1813 and the institutionalization of a conscription system are found in Dierk Walter, "Meeting the French Challenge: Conscription in Prussia, 1807–1815" (2008). He argued that this system introduced "an authoritarian rather than revolutionary approach to universal military service: a people's war without a people's army."[4] Walter and Leggiere concur that there was little long-term impact on the Prussian military system. The development of the Landwehr, concomitant with conscription, prevented political crisis in the Prussian army in terms of spreading the "disease of liberalism." Thus, the term of service for those serving in the Landwehr did not exceed the duration of the conflict. Those that fought in 1813–1814 did not serve in the Landwehr during the Waterloo Campaign in 1815.

Unlike its continental allies, Britain never resorted to conscription to fill its ranks. The British military system was a product of both the historical distrust of large standing armies, the extreme cost of maintaining one, and the primacy of naval

---

4   Dierk Walter, "Meeting the French Challenge: Conscription in Prussia, 1807–1815," in *Conscription in the Napoleonic Era: A Revolution in Military Affairs?*, eds. Donald Stoker, Frederick C. Schneid, and Harold Blanton (London: Routledge, 2009), 24–45.

power in defending the realm. Britain relied on a small professional army supplemented by allies and auxiliaries for their continental campaigns and wars abroad. This system worked well enough, until the Napoleonic Wars, and provided ample manpower for Britain's military endeavors. The classic and comprehensive account that should be consulted first is Sir John Fortescue, *A History of the British Army*, 20 vols. (1899–1926). Fortescue is not concerned with the allied or auxiliary troops but provides a highly detailed narrative history.

The number of sources available on the British army far exceeds those published on the French army. Regimental histories, military biographies, and memoirs abound. The small size of the regular army established a rather well-defined military tradition that lends itself to unit histories and memoirs. A solid, concise history is Alan Guy, ed., *The Road to Waterloo: The British Army and the Struggle against Revolutionary and Napoleonic France, 1793–1815* (1990). This broad approach to the period is important in understanding the development of the British army during this quarter century of conflict. The performance of the army from 1793 to 1808 was lackluster. The disastrous operations in Belgium and Holland during the Revolutionary Wars and the relatively mixed results during the Second Coalition necessitated change in leadership. Moreover, Britain's military efforts were divided between Europe and India. The need to enhance the strength of British forces in Europe could not be met entirely from military recruitment in Germany, a practice employed by Britain throughout the eighteenth century. Constant attempts to encourage the Russians to commit to the First Coalition were rebuffed when Catherine the Great demanded too much money for military subsidies. The response of William Wyndham Grenville, First Baron Grenville, was indicative of traditional British avenues of projecting military power: "Why should Great Britain pay the Tsarina even £300,000 when for a fraction of that sum we could hire 50,000 German mercenaries?"[5] The employment of Germans, however, ceased after 1795, and after the creation of the Rheinbund in 1806 Britain could only look to Portugal for an auxiliary force in 1808.

British regiments during the Napoleonic Wars formed a cadre to which the allied and auxiliary forces would be attached. The quality of British troops improved considerably over the course of the years, as did military leadership. Edward J. Coss's *All for the King's Shilling: The British Soldier under Wellington, 1808–1814* (2010) is an excellent examination of the British army in the Peninsular War that rejects that Wellington's British army was composed of the "scum of the earth." On the performance of the British army, despite its title, Rory Muir's *Tactics and the Experience of Battle in the Age of Napoleon* (1998) is a highly detailed tactical study of the Peninsular and Waterloo Campaigns. Readers should also consult David Gates, *The British Light Infantry Arm, 1790–1815* (1987).

The study of British military leadership has focused largely on Arthur Wellesely, the Duke of Wellington. The number of biographies and campaign histories on this man are too great to cover appropriately in this short book. Nevertheless, several important studies are recommended. Like Napoleon, Wellington did much to cultivate his legend for posterity, leaving numerous

5   John Sherwig, *Guineas and Gunpowder: British Foreign Aid in the War against France, 1793–1815* (Cambridge, MA: Harvard University Press, 1969), 22.

collections of letters, memoirs, and military dispatches. For his early campaigns abroad, Jac Weller, *Wellington in India* (1993), should be consulted. A highly anticipated study is Huw Davies, *Wellington's Wars: The Making of a Military Genius* (2012). Davies has already published several excellent articles on the use of military intelligence in the Peninsular War. For Wellington as a political general, John Severn, *Architects of Empire: The Duke of Wellington and His Brothers* (2007), is recommended. In order to understand the relationship between strategy and policy, one should consult Joshua Moon, *Wellington's Two-Front War* (2011).

Wellington was not the sum total of British military leadership during the Napoleonic Wars. One must also consider Sir John Moore and William Beresford. There are a number of nineteenth-century sources available, but no biographies of note have appeared in recent years. In regard to some of the outstanding subordinates, an analysis of Sir Thomas Picton at Buçaco appeared in Scott Hileman, "The King's Paladin" (2005). The lack of critical biographies is not surprising considering the study of individuals in history has not been well received by academia since the emergence of the Annales School.

The exploration of the British army and its leaders is only a small part of Britain's military commitment to the wars against Revolutionary and Napoleonic France. They managed a global empire and dedicated enormous financial and naval resources for its protection. The Peninsular War in Spain opened a theater of war in which their armies and naval superiority could be properly employed after the loss of continental Europe in 1807.

6   BRITAIN, SPAIN, AND THE PENINSULAR WAR

The war between Britain, France, and Spain has a special place within the historiography of the Napoleonic Wars. British and Peninsular War historians place it as a central, if not the central, event leading to the downfall of Napoleon's empire. The invasion of Spain provided Britain with a theater of war in which it could affect a direct outcome on the course of the conflict, whereas prior to 1808 it was relegated to the continental peripheries. To the Napoleonic historian who concentrates on the campaigns in central Europe, the Peninsular War was a sideshow that certainly drained French military power but did not have an immediate and direct result upon the collapse of Napoleonic hegemony. In all of this debate the Spanish history is often overlooked or subordinated to a subcategory of Britain's military efforts. The reality, however, is that for Napoleon the Peninsular War was a war on the peripheries of his empire. To Britain and Spain, it was not. For Britain, the Peninsular War was part of a global conflict that necessitated careful management of military and economic resources.

The dichotomy of the historical approach is slowly being revised to bring the three wars—continental, peninsular, and global—into a single context. This may be as successful as Einstein's search for a unified field theory; nonetheless, the perspective of the wars is entirely dependent on the location from which one is viewing the conflict. Rory Muir's outstanding study *Britain and the Defeat of Napoleon* (1996) ties the continental and Iberian wars but does not fully explore the global dimensions. Jeremy Black's two-decade attempt to force military historians to look globally has been well received, but the number of historians actually pursuing global military history, especially in terms of the Napoleonic Wars, is limited. Black's recent history of the War of 1812, *The War of 1812 in the Age of Napoleon* (2009), uses the framework of the Napoleonic Wars to inform the reader of the tremendous strain waging two simultaneous wars placed upon the British Empire. He addressed the commitment of manpower and sea power, as well as the economic and political burdens. Jonathan Riley's examination of the Napoleonic Wars, *Napoleon and the World War of 1813* (2000), as a world war equally looked at the global dimensions. A concise and extremely valuable discussion of British grand strategy is Christopher D. Hall, *British Strategy in the Napoleonic Wars, 1803–1815* (1992), and should be supplemented by Black's essay on British strategy, "British Strategy and the Struggle with France, 1793–1815" (2008).

Prior to the French Revolutionary Wars, Britain had the luxury of paying minimal attention to continental affairs in regard to its strategic security. The Bourbon-Habsburg condominium preserved a general peace, and despite tensions in the late 1780s between Austria and Prussia, and the Turkish War, Britain's policy could be focused on its overseas empire. The ongoing conquest of India absorbed resources and helped shape Britain's military leaders, particularly Arthur Wellesley in the late 1790s. A solid approach on the British campaigns in India during this period is Jac Weller, *Wellington in India* (1972). A more thorough and scholarly approach is Randolf G. Cooper, *The Anglo-Maratha Campaigns and the Contest for India* (2003), and Huw Davies, "Wellington's First Command"(2010). Perhaps one of the most significant articles that directly links Britain's conquest of India with its ability to financially survive the Napoleonic Wars is J. F. Wright, "British Government Borrowing in Wartime, 1763–1815" (1999). Wright convincingly argues that revenues derived from India floated the British economy during the Napoleonic Wars, permitting the state to economically survive in the face of Napoleon's Continental System. This article should be read in conjunction with John Sherwig, *Guineas and Gunpowder: British Foreign Aid in the War against France, 1793–1815* (1969), which clearly illustrates Britain's critical role in underwriting the many coalitions against Revolutionary and Napoleonic France.

British strategic interests extended to the Caribbean and Latin America. This part of the world had been the scene of heated competition between Britain and Spain for centuries. Again the eminent J. H. Elliott, *Empires of the Atlantic World* (2006), should be consulted. Although Spain and Britain were in an uncomfortable and strange alliance from 1793 to 1795, competition over control of Latin America was central to British policy after 1796 when Spain allied with France. The Treaty of San Il Defonso reestablished the strategic bonds that existed between France and Spain throughout much of the eighteenth century. The renewal of that alliance in 1804 placed Spain well within the Napoleonic sphere until 1808. A broad yet concise discussion that should be consulted first is John Lynch, "British Policy and Spanish America, 1783–1808" (1969). An attempt to seize Spanish colonies in South America was part of that strategy. Ian Fletcher, *Waters of Oblivion: The British Invasion of the Rio de la Plata* (1991, reprinted in 2006), provides details on the failed expedition to Argentina. Although the Spanish navy suffered severely at Trafalgar, the Spanish colonies were still capable of properly defending themselves.

Spain experienced a renaissance of colonial power in the eighteenth century as a result of policies pursued by Carlos III, including a substantial naval building program. Moreover, the late eighteenth century witnessed a recovery of silver mining that provided desperately needed funds for the state. Carlos Marichal's new history, *Bankruptcy of Empire: Mexican Silver and the Wars between Spain, Britain, and France, 1760–1810* (2007), is highly recommended. Peace on the continent between 1763 and 1789 enabled Carlos III and his successor, Carlos IV, to maintain a small standing army and pour money into the construction and maintenance of the Spanish navy. Jacques Barbier, "Indies Revenues and Naval Spending" (2007), is vital to understanding the significance of the resurrection of Spain's naval power and its impact on Britain. Similarly, John Harbron, *Trafalgar and the Spanish Navy* (1988), is largely concerned with the development of Spanish sea power prior to 1805. The strategic and historical context of the Franco-Spanish relationship through 1805 is the focus of several chapters in Schneid, *Napoleon's Conquest of Europe* (2005).

The correlation between economy and the war against France is rarely explored in terms of the continental or Peninsular campaigns, but it is a vital part of the history of the global war. The Continental System is often addressed in a separate discussion and rarely appears in campaign histories. The exception to this is Esdaile, *Napoleon's Wars*, and his essay, "De-Constructing the French Wars: Napoleon as Anti-Strategist" (2008). He views this entire period in terms of an Anglo-French conflict. Napoleonic policy, he argues, is consistently influenced by the war with Britain; the Continental System and its enforcement is center stage to the formulation of Napoleonic strategy. Prior to Esdaile, one of the first historians to address the impact of economic warfare was Francois Crouzet, "Wars, Blockade, and Economic Change in Europe, 1792–1815" (1964). Of course, the classic examination of the association of naval and state power is Alfred T. Mahan, *The Influence of Sea Power upon the French Revolution and Empire* (1892). The historical context of Mahan's work is tied to domestic arguments in the United States in the late nineteenth century for the construction of a high seas fleet to compete with Britain, France, and eventually Germany. Nonetheless, Mahan's history remains an important starting point. Jonathan Dull lately added to the discussion of naval power during this period with *The Age of the Ship of the Line: The British and French Navies, 1650–1815* (2009).

The brief Anglo-Spanish alliance (1793–1795) provided temporary cooperation between the former enemies. A joint Anglo-Spanish expedition landed at Toulon and supported the rebellious French city until its capture by Captain Napoleon Bonaparte. For the three years in which Spain and England made common cause, Britain could focus on French colonies. Michael Duffy expertly handled British operations in the Caribbean in *Soldiers, Sugar, and Seapower: The British Expeditions*

to the West Indies and the War Against Revolutionary France (1987).
The history of Haiti is tied inexorably to these events, and the
most significant account is Laurent Dubois, *Avengers of the New
World* (2004).

Britain's relative ease in seizing French colonies was aided
by the rapid decline of the French navy during the first years of
the Revolution. Understanding the implications of this decay
upon its overseas empire, the revolutionary regime dispatched
Jeanbon St. André, a member of the Committee of Public
Safety, to Brest to ensure its political and physical reconstruction. William Cormack, *Revolution and Political Conflict in the
French Navy, 1789–1794* (1995), remains the definitive source
on the revolutionary navy. After 1796, however, the Franco-
Spanish alliance challenged Britain's naval supremacy and
threatened its overseas empire. At the same time, the establishment of a pro-French republic in the Netherlands added the
Dutch navy to the anti-British coalition. The ability of
Bonaparte's expedition to sail from Toulon to Malta to Egypt
in 1798 without encountering the Royal Navy was due in large
part to strategic overstretch. Britain narrowly regained its dominance at sea with three decisive naval victories at Cape St.
Vincent (1797), Aboukir Bay (1798), and Texel (1798).

Britain's concern with maintaining its advantage at sea led
to action against European powers that were not directly involved
in the continental war. In 1801, Denmark, Sweden, Prussia,
and Russia formed the League of Armed Neutrality against
aggressive British search-and-seizure policies. Ole Feldbaek,
Denmark and Armed Neutrality, 1800–1801 (1980), discussed
the politics surrounding the formation of the league and the
preemptive strike at Copenhagen by a British fleet that ended

the alliance. The continued concern over the state of the Baltic led to a rapprochement with Sweden and an alliance lasting through 1814. Christer Jörgensen, *The Anglo-Swedish Alliance against Napoleonic France* (2004), and Tim Voelcker, *Admiral Saumarez versus Napoleon: The Baltic, 1807–1812* (2008), ably researched the development and course of this Scandinavian relationship and its significance to Sweden and Britain.

The naval history of the Napoleonic Wars is all too often separated from the rest of the historical discussion. If one ignores the global dimension this is understandable, but naval strategy was a fundamental part of British, French, and Spanish war efforts. The historiography of the British navy is quite daunting and can easily intimidate those interested tangentially in this aspect of the Napoleonic Wars. N. A. M. Rodger, the formidable historian of the Royal Navy, produced an extremely accessible and valuable article on the state of naval historiography through the Revolutionary and Napoleonic Age, "Recent Work in British Naval History" (2008). He also authored the two-volume *Command of the Ocean: A Naval History of Britain, 1649–1815* (2005). The naval successes during the War of the Second Coalition permitted Britain to send an army to Egypt in 1801. The projection of British power into the eastern Mediterranean and beyond has been the subject of substantial work by Edward Ingram in the past thirty years. Piers Mackesy produced two excellent histories of British operations in Egypt and subsequently its Mediterranean strategy during the Napoleonic Wars: *The War in the Mediterranean* (1981) and *British Victory in Egypt* (1995).

All histories of the British navy during the Napoleonic Wars must contend with Horatio Nelson. As with Wellington and

Napoleon, biographies and historical narratives abound. The key is finding the best analytical works. Roger Knight, *The Pursuit of Victory* (2005), is currently considered the most scholarly account, rejecting most of the hagiography of the past century. Nelson's ghost loomed large after his death in 1805, only adding to his legendary status. Accounts of key admirals after 1805 are few, but Kevin McCranie, *Admiral Lord Keith and the Naval War against Napoleon* (2006), is quite good, as is David Syrett, *Admiral Lord Howe* (2006). McCranie also produced a critical examination of recruitment in the Royal Navy (2009).

Britain's global war, and its expeditions on the continental peripheries, ended in 1808 with the initiation of the Peninsular War. The French invasion of Portugal in 1807, followed by the seizure of power in Spain, provided Britain with a theater of war, and the allied and auxiliary manpower it lost in Central Europe after 1795. The Peninsular War therefore is center stage in the Anglo-French dimension of the Napoleonic Wars, between 1808 and 1814. It is also here that Arthur Wellesley cemented his reputation, which earned him a promotion in rank and title.

The French invasion of Portugal in 1807, prior to the Napoleonic coup in Spain, offered the first glimpse into the future Anglo-French conflict. This was the second time the small Iberian state fell victim to Napoleonic policy. In 1801, Portugal maintained its close economic and political ties to Britain. Napoleon prepared a small expeditionary force but succeeded in convincing the Spanish to conduct a campaign instead. The short "War of Oranges" compelled Portugal to abandon its relationship with England. Schneid, *Napoleon's Conquest of Europe* (2005), provides some discussion on this brief conflict. The conclusion of the Peace of Amiens in 1802 led to the restoration of Anglo-Portuguese relations. As in 1801, the Portuguese could not properly defend their kingdom, and French occupation followed. A short and brilliant campaign by Wellesley led to the surrender of the entire French force in Portugal in 1808. From this moment, the Anglo-Portuguese strategic alliance became the key to the exportation of British power on the continent. Unfortunately, the development of this relationship was threatened by the French occupation of Spain.

Almost six months after the French invasion of Spain a British expedition landed at Corunna under Gen. Sir John Moore, but it ended with disastrous results. The return of Wellesley, now the Duke of Wellington, opened a new phase in the Peninsular and Napoleonic Wars. The subsequent war of attrition conducted by Wellington and his Spanish allies fared much better. The two standard multivolume histories of the Peninsular War from 1807 to 1814 are William Francis Napier, *History of the War in the Peninsula*, 4 vols. (1828–1840), and Sir Charles Oman, *A History of the Peninsular War*, 7 vols. (1902–1930). Napier served as an officer in the Peninsular War, and his analysis is decidedly biased against many of his British contemporaries. His history is rather sympathetic to Napoleon and his marshals. Charles Oman, the eminent British military historian, sought to address Napier's biases and place the campaigns in their proper historical and military context. His history is narrative in approach, but it is a treasure trove. Both Oman and Napier provide a wealth of information on the British and French campaigns but do not spend much time on the Spanish, except as British auxiliaries, and only a bit on the bitter guerrilla war.

In the late 1980s David Gates and Charles Esdaile introduced two histories that shaped current views of the conflict in the Iberian Peninsula. Gates, *The Spanish Ulcer* (1986), condensed the Peninsular War into a single volume, integrating scholarship since the publication of Oman's books. Gates, however, remained focused on the conventional campaigns and sieges, with the British and French accounts at center stage. To that end, Donald Horward provided three valuable histories of the French military efforts in Portugal: *The Battle of Bussaco* (1965), a translation of Jacques Pelet's *French Campaign in Portugal* (1973), and a history of the twin sieges of Ciudad Rodrigo and Almeida, *Napoleon and Iberia* (1984). These also fell into the range of traditional campaign narratives. Esdaile, however, altered perceptions of the Peninsular War by exploring the relationship between the British and Spanish armies. His first books, *The Spanish Army in the Peninsular War* (1988) and *The Duke of Wellington and the Command of the Spanish Army* (1990), introduced a new historical dimension in English-language historiography.

Esdaile has single-handedly moved the historical discussion away from the monolithic Napier and Oman to a fully integrated history that incorporates the Spanish army, the guerrillas, the British, French, and Portuguese in *The Peninsular War: A New History* (2003). Historians are forced to contend with his arguments as a consequence of the scholarship. Perhaps his most contentious work is tied to his research on the guerrillas. The role of guerrilla warfare in the defeat of Napoleon's armies forms a particularly critical school of thought in Spanish historiography. The Peninsular War is referred to as the "War of Independence" in Spain, and the guerrilla is perceived in popular culture as an equivalent of the "minuteman" in American history. Popular resistance to the Napoleonic regime is accepted as a fundamental part of Spanish history. Esdaile took the history of the Spanish guerrilla head-on in *Fighting Napoleon: Guerrillas, Bandits and Adventurers in Spain, 1808–1814* (2004). A highly revisionist work, *Fighting Napoleon* rejects the nationalist myth of the guerrilla and provides a more complex analysis than previous histories. The guerrilla was a manifestation of either former soldiers and units remaining from the broken Spanish army or bands of brigands that existed prior to the French invasion that continued their activities afterward. Esdaile contends that the concept of the Spanish guerrilla was manufactured in part by the state, by Wellington, and by local legend. Needless to say, his revisionism has made him a ripe target for Peninsular War and Spanish historians alike.

One of the earlier regional histories of the guerrillas is John Tone, *The Fatal Knot: The Guerrilla War in Navarre and the Defeat of Napoleon in Spain* (1994). Esdaile considers Tone's book on the Navarrese guerrillas "the most detailed work in the English language" but ultimately rejects Tone's overarching analysis and conclusions, which he believes fall into the category of traditional historiography of the guerrillas. Nevertheless, regional studies of the guerrillas continue to receive notice from Napoleonic historians. Don W. Alexander, *Rod of Iron: French Counterinsurgency Policy in Aragon during the Peninsular War* (1985), is quite good on French response to asymmetric warfare. Recently the scholarship of John Morgan, "War Feeding War?"(2009), introduced a detailed archival view of the impact of the guerrilla war on French occupation policy and operations.

The strategic and operational history of the Peninsular War found new life in the works above. The battle histories of the Peninsular War are numerous, and those in English are written decidedly from the British perspective. This bias is due to the enormous literature produced in Britain in the past two centuries. Much of these histories are battle narratives, with little analysis or a preference for the narrator as "armchair general." Two books of note, however, have appeared in the past decade that do well to introduce students of operational and tactical history to a new approach in this field. Rory Muir, *Salamanca 1812* (2001), preceded by his study of tactics, *Britain and the Defeat of Napoleon* (1996). The battle of Salamanca served as a turning point in the Peninsular War, as Wellington thoroughly defeated one of the major French armies under Marshal Auguste de Marmont. All of this was done while Napoleon was marching on Moscow. The battle is viewed from both British and French perspectives, with a particular interest in the soldier's experience. Muir picked up where John Keegan, *The Face of Battle* (1976), left off, exploring war from the soldier's perspective. A more critical battle analysis that is highly recommended is Guy Dempsey, *Albuera 1811* (2008). Dempsey is interested in the battle as a comparison of military systems and leadership. The Anglo-Spanish-Portuguese Army at Albuera was not under the command of the Duke of Wellington but Lord Beresford. Marshal Nicholas Soult, considered to be among the first rank of Napoleon's lieutenants, ably led the French army. Dempsey interprets the battle as a result of wills, skills, and tactics. He consulted French and British archival sources in addition to a host of memoirs and narratives.

It is clear from this brief discussion of the British war effort that opportunities abound for the researcher. Regarding the Peninsular War, one must consider Charles Esdaile the foremost scholar who altered the course of Peninsular War historiography.

His arguments remain contentious and will fuel further debate and encourage deeper research into guerrillas, the Spanish army, and Anglo-Spanish cooperation. More, too, is needed on the Portuguese. The most promising opportunities, however, are in the exploration of the global dimensions of the war against France. Trans-Atlantic and transnational histories are currently the trend in university scholarship, but military history is by nature transnational. A historian who is willing to move across the Atlantic and utilize recent research on Latin American military developments during the Revolutionary and Napoleonic Era will find ground as fertile as the Anglo-Indian military relationship during this period.

CONCLUSION

The Napoleonic Wars left an indelible mark on warfare at all levels. The organization, administration, composition, and conduct of armies changed considerably after this period. It was certainly the birth of modern warfare in the sense of national conscription, the development of the general staff system, and the ability of states to achieve decisive victories over their opponents. Nonetheless, the scope of the Napoleonic Wars, and the implications of national war on a Europe that remained monarchical and anti-constitutional, meant that the application of those lessons would be limited. If war was the "sport of kings" and pursued on the principles of raison d'état prior to 1789, then war must be restrained after 1815. In common understanding, the Congress of Vienna (1814–1815), the peace conference at the end of the Napoleonic Wars, established the principle of the "balance of power." All agreed that no European state should threaten to dominate the continent as France had done. Paul Schroeder, "Did the Vienna System Rest Upon a Balance of Power?" (1992), challenged our understanding of the congress, defining it more properly as new rules for the expansion of hegemonic powers without threatening the general peace in Europe.

The diplomatic ramifications of the Napoleonic Wars paralleled the military response. Despite the institution of universal conscription in France, and the adaption of modified forms of recruitment throughout Europe, no European state maintained these systems after the war. The French government rejected universal conscription in favor of a limited method as explained by Thomas Hippler, *Citizens, Soldiers and National Armies* (2008), while the Landwehr, so critical to Prussian military power after 1813, was eliminated by 1819. Military service combined with revolutionary movements provided a dangerous mixture, and European governments purged their armed forces by 1820–1821 of this potential danger. Schneid, "Conscription and the Militarization of Europe" (2009), rejected the notion that a decade of conscription militarized European society. Traditional recruitment and selective conscription remained the order of the day through 1848.

Despite the rejection of the most controversial and politically dangerous elements of Napoleonic warfare, European states gradually adopted the higher organization of army, corps, and divisions. A general staff system evolved along a French or Prussian model, although the former had greater influence in the first half of the nineteenth century. The campaigns of Napoleon were studied at war colleges throughout Europe and at West Point. Robert E. Lee actively participated in the Napoleon club at the U.S. Military Academy in the 1820s. At the same time Helmuth von Moltke, the future chief of the Prussian and German general staffs, attended the Prussian War College, headed by Clausewitz. Lastly, in most countries all the senior officers and many junior officers who held commissions through mid-century and beyond had served in the Napoleonic Wars. In France the emergence of the Second French Empire in 1851 under Napoleon III, nephew of the former emperor, found a relatively easy transition as the sons of the marshals and generals of the First Empire were the senior officers of the French army at the birth of the Second Empire.

Napoleonic strategy dominated military thought. Although few wars were fought in Europe during the nineteenth century, all reflected a clear Napoleonic influence. During the War of Italian Unification (1859–1861) French, Piedmontese, and Austrian general staffs commonly referred to Napoleon's campaign in northern Italy in 1796. Jomini provided military advice to Napoleon III, and the Austrian commander moved cautiously, fearing a repeat of Bonaparte's famous *manoeuvre sur les derrière* that chased his predecessors from Lombardy more than a half century earlier. The Wars of German Unification (1859–1871) exhibited Napoleonic principles drawn from the lessons of 1813. The concentric advance of armies upon a central point led to coalition victory at Leipzig in 1813. The same principles led to Prussia's victory over Austria at Königgrätz in 1866 and over France at Sedan in 1870. The irony was that the two most revolutionary factors that changed the face of war in the nineteenth century had nothing to do with Napoleon. The industrial revolution and the age of imperialism profoundly altered the scope, capacity, and application of European military power on a global scale. The Napoleonic Wars found a home at the military academies, but the application of Napoleonic strategy combined with the new realities of the industrial age were not fully realized until the First World War.

SELECTED BIBLIOGRAPHY

Preface

Caldwell, Ronald J. *The Era of Napoleon: A Bibliography of the History of Western Civilization, 1799–1815*. New York: Garland, 1991.
Horward, Donald, ed. *Napoleonic Military History: A Bibliography*. New York: Garland, 1986.

Introduction

Clausewitz, Carl von. *On War*. Edited and translated by Michael Howard and Peter Paret. Princeton, NJ: Princeton University Press, 1976.
———. *The Campaign of 1812 in Russia*. Philadelphia: Da Capo Press, 1995.
Jomini, Antoine-Henri, Baron de. *The Art of War*. Edited and translated by G. H. Mendell and W. P. Craighill. Philadelphia: J.P. Lippincott, 1862.
Paret, Peter. "Napoleon and the Revolution in War." In *Makers of Modern Strategy: From Machiavelli to the Nuclear Age*, edited by Peter Paret. Princeton, NJ: Princeton University Press, 1986.
Tarlé, Eugene. *Napoleon's Invasion of Russia 1812*. New York: Oxford University Press, 1942.

Chapter 1: The Origins of Napoleonic Warfare

Aksan, Virginia. *Ottoman Wars 1700–1870: An Empire Besieged.* Harlow, UK: Longman, 2007.

Arnold, James. "A Reappraisal of Column Versus Line in the Peninsular War." *Journal of Military History* 68, no. 2 (April 2004): 535–52.

———. *Marengo and Hohenlinden: Napoleon's Rise to Power.* Barnsley, UK: Pen and Sword, 2005.

Bell, David A. *The First Total War: Napoleon's Europe and the Birth of Warfare As We Know It.* New York: Houghton Mifflin, 2007.

Bertaud, Jean-Paul. *The Army of the French Revolution: From Citizen-Soldiers to Instrument of Power.* Princeton, NJ: Princeton University Press, 1988.

Bien, David. "The Army in the French Enlightenment: Reform, Reaction and Revolution." *Past & Present* 85 (November 1979): 68–98.

Black, Jeremy. "British Strategy and the Struggle with France, 1793–1815." *Journal of Strategic Studies* 31, no. 4 (August 2008): 553–69.

———. "Eighteenth Century Warfare Reconsidered." *War in History* 1, no. 2 (1994): 215–32.

Blanning, T. C. W. *The French Revolutionary Wars, 1787–1802.* London: Arnold, 1996.

———. *The Origins of the French Revolutionary Wars.* London: Longman, 1986.

Boycott-Brown, Martin. *The Road to Rivoli: Napoleon's First Campaign.* London: Casell, 2001.

Brown, Howard. *War, Revolution, and the Bureaucratic State: Politics and Army Administration in France, 1791–1799.* New York: Oxford University Press, 1995.

Bruce, Robert, Iain Dickie, Kevin Kiley, Michael F. Pavkovic, and Frederick C. Schneid. *Fighting Techniques of the Napoleonic Age, 1792–1815: Equipment, Combat Skills, and Tactics.* New York: St. Martin's Press, 2008.

Chandler, David G. *The Campaigns of Napoleon: The Mind and Method of History's Greatest Soldier.* New York: Macmillan, 1966.

Cole, Juan. *Napoleon's Egypt: Invading the Middle East.* New York: Palgrave Macmillan, 2007.

Connelly, Owen. *Blundering to Glory: Napoleon's Military Campaigns.* Wilmington, DE: Scholarly Resources, 1987.

———. "Forum: French Army, 1789–1815." *French Historical Studies* 16, no. 1 (Spring 1989): 152–82.

Elliott, J. H. *Empires of the Atlantic World: Britain and Spain in America, 1492–1830.* New Haven, CT: Yale University Press, 2006.

Esdaile, Charles. *Napoleon's Wars: An International History, 1803–1815.* London: Allen Lane, 2007.

Eysturlid, Lee. *The Formative Influences, Theories, and Campaigns of the Archduke Carl of Austria.* Westport, CT: Greenwood Press, 2000.

Ferrero, Guglielmo. *The Gamble: Bonaparte in Italy, 1796–1797.* New York: Walker & Co., 1961.

Forrest, Alan. *The Soldiers of the French Revolution.* Durham, NC: Duke University Press, 1990.

Fortescue, Sir John. *A History of the British Army.* 13 vols. London: Macmillan, 1899–1930.

Goetz, Robert. *1805, Austerlitz: Napoleon and the Destruction of the Third Coalition.* London: Greenhill Books, 2005.

Griffith, Paddy. *The Art of War of Revolutionary France, 1789–1802.* London: Greenhill Books, 1998.

Hochedlinger, Michael. "Who's Afraid of the French Revolution: Austrian Foreign Policy and the European Crisis 1787–1797." *German History* 21, no. 3 (2003): 293–318.

Kagan, Frederick. *The End of the Old Order: Napoleon and Europe, 1801–1805.* Philadelphia: Da Capo Press, 2005.

Liaropoulos, Andrew. "Revolutions in Warfare: Theoretical Paradigms and Historical Evidence—The Napoleonic and First World War Revolutions in Military Affairs." *Journal of Military History* 70, no. 2 (April 2006): 363–84.

Lynn, John. *The Bayonets of the Republic: Motivation and Tactics in the Army of Revolutionary France, 1791–1794.* Boulder, CO: Westview Press, 1996. First published in 1984 by University of Illinois Press.

———. "Toward an Army of Honor: The Moral Evolution of the French Army, 1789–1815." *French Historical Studies* 16, no. 1 (Spring 1989): 152–73.

Moiret, Joseph-Marie. *The Memoirs of Napoleon's Egyptian Expedition.* Barnsley, UK: Greenhill Books, 2006.

Muir, Rory. *Tactics and the Experience of Battle in the Age of Napoleon.* New Haven, CT: Yale University Press, 1998.

Oman, Charles. *Column and Line in the Peninsular War.* Oxford, UK: Oxford University Press, 1910.

Paret, Peter. *Cognitive Challenge of War: Prussia 1806.* Princeton, NJ: Princeton University Press, 2009.

———. "Napoleon and the Revolution in War." In *Makers of Modern Strategy: From Machiavelli to the Nuclear Age*, edited by Peter Paret. Princeton, NJ: Princeton University Press, 1986.

———. *Yorck and the Era of Prussian Reform, 1807–1815.* Princeton, NJ: Princeton University Press, 1966.

Parker, Harold T. "Napoleon and French Army Values." Western Society for French History Proceedings, 1991.

Phipps, Ramsay Weston. *The Armies of the First French Republic and the Rise of the Marshals of Napoleon I.* 5 vols. Oxford: Oxford University Press, 1926–1935.

Quimby, Robert. *The Background of Napoleonic Warfare: The Theory of Military Tactics in Eighteenth-Century France.* New York: Columbia University Press, 1952.

Rodger, A. B. *The War of the Second Coalition, 1798–1801, a Strategic Commentary.* Oxford: Clarendon Press, 1964.

Roider, Karl. *Baron Thugut and Austria's Response to the French Revolution.* Princeton, NJ: Princeton University Press, 1987.

Rothenberg, Gunther E. *The Art of Warfare in the Age of Napoleon.* Bloomington: Indiana University Press, 1976.

———. "The Origins, Causes and Extensions of the Wars of the French Revolution and Napoleon." *Journal of Interdisciplinary History* 18 (1988): 77–193.

———. *Napoleon's Great Adversaries: The Archduke Charles and the Austrian Army, 1792–1814.* Bloomington: Indiana University Press, 1982.

———. *Napoleonic Wars.* London: Cassell, 1999.

Schneid, Frederick C., ed. *Armies of the French Revolution.* Norman: University of Oklahoma Press (forthcoming).

———. "The Grand Strategy of the Habsburg Monarchy during the War of the Third Coalition." *Selected Papers 2007 of the Consortium on the Revolutionary Era, 1750–1850* (2008): 313–21.

———, ed. *Warfare in Europe 1792–1815.* Aldershot, UK: Ashgate, 2007.

Schroeder, Paul. "The Collapse of the Second Coalition." *Journal of Modern History* 59, no. 2 (June 1987): 244–90.

———. "Did the Vienna System Rest Upon a Balance of Power." *American Historical Review* 97 (1992): 683–706.

———. *The Transformation of European Politics, 1763–1848*. New York: Oxford University Press, 1994.

Schur, Nathan. *Napoleon in the Holy Land*. Barnsley, UK: Greenhill Books, 2006.

Scott, Samuel F. *From Yorktown to Valmy: The Transformation of the French Army in an Age of Revolution*. Denver: University of Colorado Press, 1998.

———. *The Response of the Royal Army to the French Revolution: The Role and Development of the Line Army, 1787–1793*. Oxford: Clarendon Press, 1978.

Szabo, Franz. *The Seven Years War in Europe, 1756–1763*. New York: Longman, 2008.

Tignor, Robert, and Shmuel Moreh. *Napoleon in Egypt: Al-Jabarti's Chronicle of the First Seven Months of the French Occupation, 1798*. Princeton, NJ: Markus Wiener Publishing, 2003.

Wilkinson, Spenser. *The Defence of Piedmont, 1742–1748: A Prelude to the Study of Napoleon*. Oxford: Clarendon Press, 1927.

———. *The French Army before Napoleon: Lectures Delivered before the University of Oxford in Michaelmas Term, 1914*. Oxford: Clarendon Press, 1915.

———. *The Rise of General Bonaparte*. Oxford: Clarendon Press, 1930.

Chapter 2: The Napoleonic Wars

Black, Jeremy. "British Strategy and the Struggle with France, 1793–1815." *Journal of Strategic Studies* 21, no. 4 (August 2008): 553–69.

Chandler, David. *The Campaigns of Napoleon: The Mind and Method of History's Greatest Soldier*. New York: Macmillan, 1966.

Connelly, Owen. *Blundering to Glory: Napoleon's Military Campaigns*. Wilmington, DE: Scholarly Resources, 1987.

———. *The Wars of the French Revolution and Napoleon, 1792–1815*. London: Routledge, 2005.

Dwyer, Philip. "Self-Interest versus the Common Cause: Austria, Prussia and Russia against Napoleon." *Journal of Strategic Studies* 21, no. 4 (August 2008): 605–32.

Esdaile, Charles. "De-Constructing the French Wars: Napoleon as Anti-Strategist." *Journal of Strategic Studies* 21, no. 4 (August 2008): 515–52.

———. *The Napoleonic Wars: An International History, 1803–1815.* London: Allen Lane, 2007.

———. *The Wars of Napoleon.* New York: Longman, 1995.

Gates, David. *The Napoleonic Wars, 1803–1815.* London: Arnold, 1997.

Harvey, Robert. *The War of Wars: The Great European Conflict, 1793–1815.* New York: Carroll & Graf, 2006.

Loraine, Petre, F. *Napoleon and the Archduke Charles.* London: John Lane, 1909.

———. *Napoleon at Bay, 1814.* London: John Lane, 1913.

———. *Napoleon's Campaign in Poland, 1806–1807.* London: Sampson Low & Co., 1901.

———. *Napoleon's Conquest of Prussia, 1806.* London: John Lane, 1907.

———. *Napoleon's Last Campaign in Germany, 1813.* London: John Lane, 1912.

Paret, Peter. "The Annales School and the History of War." *Journal of Military History* 73, no. 4 (October 2009): 1289–94.

Riley, Jonathon. *Napoleon as a General: Command from the Battlefield to Grand Strategy.* London: Hambeldon, 2007.

Rothenberg, Gunther E. *The Art of Warfare in the Age of Napoleon.* Bloomington: Indiana University Press, 1976.

———. *The Napoleonic Wars.* London: Cassell, 1999.

Schneid, Frederick C. "Kings, Clients and Satellites in the Napoleonic Imperium." *Journal of Strategic Studies* 21, no. 4 (August 2008): 571–604.

———, ed. *Warfare in Europe, 1792–1815.* Ashgate: Aldershot, 2007.

Chapter 3: The Campaigns

Arnold, James R., and Ralph R. Reinertsen. *Crisis in the Snows: Russia Confronts Napoleon: The Eylau Campaign 1806–1807.* Lexington, VA: Napoleon Books, 2007.

Austin, Paul Britten. *1812: Napoleon's Invasion of Russia.* London: Greenhill Books, 2000.

———. *1812: The Great Retreat*. London: Greenhill Books, 1996.

Barbero, Alessandro. *The Battle: A New History of Waterloo*. New York: Walker & Company, 2006.

Black, Jeremy. *The Battle of Waterloo*. New York: Random House, 2010.

———. *The War of 1812 in the Age of Napoleon*. Norman: University of Oklahoma Press, 2009.

Bourgogne, Adrien Jean Baptiste François. *The Memoirs of Sergeant Bourgogne, 1812–1813*. Edited by Paul Cottin. New York: Hippocrene Books, 1979.

Bowden Scott, ed. *Napoleon's Finest: Davout and His 3rd Corps. Combat Journal of Operations, 1805–1807*. Chicago: Emperor's Press, 2006.

Broers, Michael. *Napoleon's Other War: Bandits, Rebels and their Pursuers in the Age of Revolutions*. Witney, UK: Peter Lang, 2010.

Cate, Curtis. *The War of Two Emperors: The Duel between Napoleon and Alexander—Russia, 1812*. New York: Random House, 1985.

Caulaincourt, Armand-Augustin-Louis de. *With Napoleon in Russia: The Memoirs of General de Caulaincourt, Duke of Vicenza*. New York: William Morrow, 1935.

Chandler, David. *Campaigns of Napoleon: The Mind and Method of History's Greatest Soldier*. New York: Macmillan, 1966.

Clausewitz, Carl von. *The Campaign of 1812 in Russia*. London: Greenhill Books, 1992. First published in 1843. Translated by anonymous.

Cook, Llewellyn. "Command in Crisis: The Army of Bohemia, May–August 1813." *Selected Papers of the Consortium on the Revolutionary Era* (2008): 215–25.

Craig, Gordon. "Problems of Coalition Warfare: The Military Alliance against Napoleon, 1813–1814." In *War, Politics, and Diplomacy: Selected Essays by Gordon Craig*. Westport, CT: Praeger, 1966.

Davydov, Denis. *In the Service of the Tsar against Napoleon: The Memoirs of Denis Davydov, 1806–1814*. Edited and translated by Gregory Troubetzkoy. Barnsley, UK: Greenhill Books, 2006.

Duffy, Christopher. *Austerlitz 1805*. London: Seeley Service & Co., Ltd., 1977.

———. *Borodino and the War of 1812*. London: Seeley Service & Co., Ltd., 1972.

Dwyer, Philip. "Self-Interest versus the Common Cause: Austria, Prussia and Russia against Napoleon." *Journal of Strategic Studies* 21, no. 4 (August 2008): 605–32.

Epstein, Robert. *Napoleon's Last Victory and the Emergence of Modern War*. Lawrence: University of Kansas Press, 1994.

Ermolov, Alexis. *The Czar's General: The Memoirs of a Russian General in the Napoleonic Wars*. Edited and translated by Alexander Mikaberidze. Welwyn Garden City, UK: Ravenhall, 2005.

Esdaile, Charles, ed. *Popular Resistance in the French Wars: Patriots, Partisans and Land Pirates*. New York: Palgrave Macmillan, 2005.

Eyck, F. Gunther. *Loyal Rebels: Andreas Hofer and the Tyrolean Uprising of 1809*. Lanham, MD: University Press of America, 1986.

Finley, Milton. *The Most Monstrous of Wars: The Napoleonic Guerrilla War in Southern Italy, 1806–1811*. Columbia: University of South Carolina Press, 1994.

Flayhart, William. *Counterpoint to Trafalgar: The Anglo-Russian Invasion of Naples, 1805–1806*. Columbia: University of South Carolina Press, 1992.

Gill, John H. *1809: Thunder on the Danube: Napoleon's Defeat of the Habsburgs*. 3 vols. London: Frontline Books, 2008–2010.

———. *With Eagles to Glory: Napoleon and His German Allies in the 1809 Campaign*. London: Greenhill Books, 1992.

Goetz, Robert. *1805, Austerlitz: Napoleon and the Destruction of the Third Coalition*. London: Greenhill Books, 2005.

Hofschroer, Peter. *1815, the Waterloo Campaign: Wellington, His German Allies and the Battles of Ligny and Quatre Bras*. Barnsley, UK: Greenhill, 2006.

Houssaye, Henry. *1815, Waterloo*. Translated by Arthur Emil Manne. London: Adam & Charles Black, 1900.

Kagan, Frederick W. *The End of the Old Order: Napoleon and Europe, 1801–1805*. Philadelphia: Da Capo Press, 2005.

Leggiere, Michael V. "Austrian Grand Strategy and the Invasion of France in 1814." *Selected Papers of the Consortium on the Revolutionary Era* (2007): 322–31.

———. *The Fall of Napoleon: The Allied Invasion of France 1813–1814*. Cambridge: Cambridge University Press, 2007.

———. *Napoleon and Berlin: The Franco-Prussian War in North Germany, 1813*. Norman: University of Oklahoma Press, 2002.

Lieven, Dominic. *Russia Against Napoleon: The True Story of the Campaigns of War and Peace*. New York: Viking, 2010.

Loraine, Petre F. *Napoleon and the Archduke Charles*. London: John Lane, 1909.

———. *Napoleon at Bay—1814*. London: John Lane, 1913.

———. *Napoleon's Campaign in Poland, 1806–1807*. London: Sampson Low & Co., 1901.

———. *Napoleon's Conquest of Prussia—1806*. London: John Lane, 1907.

———. *Napoleon's Last Campaign in Germany—1813*. London: John Lane, 1912.

Maude, F. N. *The Jena Campaign, 1806*. London: Greenhill Books, 1998. First published in 1909 by Macmillan.

———. *Ulm: The Campaign of 1805*. Leonaur, 2008.

Mikaberidze, Alexander. *The Battle of the Berezina: Napoleon's Great Escape*. Barnsley, UK: Pen & Sword, 2010.

———. *The Battle of Borodino: Napoleon Against Kutuzov*. Barnsley, UK: Pen & Sword, 2007.

———. "The Conflict of Command in the Russian Army in 1812." *Selected Papers of the Consortium on Revolutionary Europe* (2002): 314–25.

Mustafa, Sam. *The Long Ride of Major von Schill: A Journey through German History and Memory*. Lanham, MD: Rowman & Littlefield, 2008.

Nofi, Albert. *Napoleon at War: Selected Writings of F. Loraine Petre*. New York: Hippocrene Books, 1984.

Paret, Peter. *The Cognitive Challenge of War: Prussia 1806*. Princeton, NJ: Princeton University Press, 2009.

Riehn, Richard K. *1812: Napoleon's Russian Campaign*. New York: McGraw-Hill, 1990.

Riley, Jonathon P. *Napoleon and the World War of 1813: Lessons in Coalition Warfighting*. London: Frank Cass, 2000.

Rothenberg, Gunther E. *The Emperor's Last Victory: Napoleon and the Battle of Wagram*. London: Weidenfeld & Nicolson, 2004.

———. *Napoleon's Great Adversary: The Archduke Charles and the Austrian Army, 1792–1814*. Bloomington: Indiana University Press, 1982.

Schneid, Frederick C. "The Dynamics of Defeat: French Army Leadership, December 1812–March 1813." *Journal of Military History* 63, no. 1 (January 1999): 7–28.

————. *Napoleon's Conquest of Europe: The War of the Third Coalition.* Westport, CT: Praeger, 2005.

————. *Napoleon's Italian Campaigns, 1805–1815.* Westport, CT: Praeger, 2002.

Ségur, Philippe de. *Napoleon's Russian Campaign.* Boston: Houghton Mifflin, 1958.

Showalter, Dennis. "Hubertusberg to Auerstädt: The Prussian Army in Decline?" *German History* 12 (1994): 308–30.

————. "Reform and Stability: Prussia's Military Dialectic From Hubertusberg to Waterloo." In *The Projection and Limitations of Imperial Powers*, edited by Frederick C. Schneid. Leiden, the Netherlands: Brill, 2012.

Siborne, William. *History of the Waterloo Campaign.* London: Greenhill Books, 1990. First published in 1844 by T. and W. Boone.

Tarlé, Eugene. *Napoleon's Invasion of Russia, 1812.* New York: Oxford University Press, 1942.

Uffindel, Andrew. *The Eagle's Last Triumph: Napoleon's Victory at Ligny, June 1815.* London: Greenhill Books, 2006.

Walter, Jakob. *The Diary of a Napoleonic Foot Soldier.* New York: Doubleday, 1991.

Zamoyski, Adam. *Moscow 1812: Napoleon's Fatal March.* New York: HarperCollins, 2004.

Chapter 4: Satellites and Minor States: Puppets or Independent Actors?

Aksan, Virginia. *Ottoman Wars 1700–1870: An Empire Besieged.* Harlow, UK: Longman, 2007.

Broers, Michael. *Napoleon's Other War: Bandits, Rebels and Their Pursuers in the Age of Revolutions.* Witney, UK: Peter Lang, 2010.

Connelly, Owen. *Napoleon's Satellite Kingdoms.* New York: Free Press, 1965.

Czubaty, Jarosław. "Army of the Duchy of Warsaw." In Gregorgy Fremont-Barnes. *Armies of the Napoleonic Wars.* Barnsley, UK: Pen & Sword, 2011.

Della Peruta, Franco. "War and Society in Napoleonic Italy: The Armies of the Kingdom of Italy at Home and Abroad." In *Society and Politics in the Age of the Risorgimento*, edited by John A. Davis and Paul Ginsborg. Cambridge: Cambridge University Press, 1991.

Elting, John. *Swords Around A Throne: Napoleon's Grande Armée*. New York: Free Press, 1988.

Esdaile, Charles, ed. *Popular Resistance in the French Wars: Patriots, Partisans and Land Pirates*. New York: Palgrave Macmillan, 2005.

Finley, Milton. *The Most Monstrous of Wars: The Napoleonic Guerrilla War in Southern Italy, 1806–1811*. Columbia: University of South Carolina Press, 1994.

Flayhart, William. *Counterpoint to Trafalgar: The Anglo-Russian Invasion of Naples, 1805–1806*. Columbia: University of South Carolina Press, 1992.

Gill, John H. *1809 Thunder on the Danube: Napoleon's Defeat of the Habsburgs*. 3 vols. London: Frontline Books, 2008–2010.

———. "Vermin, Scorpions, and Mosquitoes: The *Rheinbund* in the Peninsula." In *The Peninsular War: Aspects of the Struggle for the Iberian Peninsula*, edited by Ian Fletcher. Staplehurst, UK: Spellmount, 1998.

———. *With Eagles to Glory: Napoleon and His German Allies in the 1809 Campaign*. London: Greenhill Books, 1992.

Grab, Alexander. "Army, State and Society: Conscription and Desertion in Napoleonic Italy, 1802–1814." *Journal of Modern History* 67 (1995): 25–54.

———. "Conscription and Desertion in Napoleonic Italy, 1802–1814." In *Conscription in the Napoleonic Era: A Revolution in Military Affairs?*, edited by Donald Stoker, Frederick C. Schneid, and Harold Blanton. London: Routledge, 2009.

———. "State Power, Brigandage and Rural Resistance in Napoleonic Italy." *European History Quarterly* 25, no. 1 (1995): 39–70.

Hattem, Mark van, and Mariska Pool. "Four Men and a Woman: Remarkable Dutch Experiences during the Russian Campaign of Napoleon in 1812." *Selected Papers of the Consortium on the Revolutionary Era, 1750–1850* (2008): 245–60.

———. *In the Wake of Napoleon: The Dutch in Time of War, 1792–1815*. Bussum, the Netherlands: Army Museum, 2006.

Ilari, Virgilio, and Giancarlo Boeri. *Le Due Sicile nelle Guerre Napoleoniche (1800–1815)*. Rome: USSME, 2009.

Ilari, Virgilio, Ciro Paoletti, and Piero Croaciani. *Storia Militare del Regno Italico (1802–1814)*. Rome: USMME, 2004.

Jörgensen, Christer. *The Anglo-Swedish Alliance against Napoleonic France*. New York: Palgrave Macmillan, 2004.

Klang, Daniel. "Bavaria and the War of Liberation." *French Historical Studies* 4, no. 1 (Spring 1965): 22–41.

Lamar, Glenn. *Jerome Bonaparte: The War Years, 1800–1815*. Westport, CT: Greenwood, 2000.

Leggiere, Michael V. *Napoleon and Berlin: The Franco-Prussian War in North Germany, 1813*. Norman: University of Oklahoma Press, 2002.

———. *The Fall of Napoleon: The Allied Invasion of France, 1813–1814*. Cambridge: Cambridge University Press, 2007.

Mikaberidze, Alexander. *The Battle of the Berezina: Napoleon's Great Escape*. Barnsley, UK: Pen & Sword, 2010.

Pavkovic, Michael. "Recruitment and Conscription in the Kingdom of Westphalia: The Palladium of Westphalian Freedom." In *Conscription in the Napoleonic Era: A Revolution in Military Affairs?*, edited by Donald Stoker, Frederick Schneid, and Harold Blanton. London: Routledge, 2009.

Rothenberg, Gunther E. "A Massachusetts Yankee in Elector Karl Theodor's Court: Benjamin Thompson, Count Rumford in the Palitinate-Bavarian Service." *Selected Papers 2004 of the Consortium on Revolutionary Europe, 1750–1850* (2008): 1–15.

Sauzey, Jean. *Les Allemandes sous les Aigles Française: Essai sur les Troupes de la Confédération du Rhin, 1806–1814*. 6 vols. Paris: C. Terana, 1902–1912.

Schama, Simon. *Patriots and Liberators: Revolution in the Netherlands, 1780–1813*. New York: Vintage Books, 1992.

Schneid, Frederick C. "Army of the Kingdom of Italy." In *Armies of the Napoleonic Wars*, edited by Gregory Fremont-Barnes. Barnsley, UK: Pen & Sword, 2011.

———. "Kings, Clients and Satellites in the Napoleonic Imperium." *Journal of Strategic Studies* 1, no. 4 (August 2008): 571–604.

———. *Napoleon's Conquest of Europe: The War of the Third Coalition*. Westport, CT: Praeger, 2005.

———. *Napoleon's Italian Campaigns, 1805–1815*. Westport, CT: Praeger, 2002.

———. *Soldiers of Napoleon's Kingdom of Italy: Army, State, and Society, 1800–1815*. Boulder, CO: Westview Press, 1995.

Thisner, Fredrik. "Manning the armed forces: The Swedish Solution." In *Conscription in the Napoleonic Era: A Revolution in Military*

Affairs?, edited by Donald Stoker, Frederick C. Schneid, and Harold Blanton. London: Routledge, 2009.

Wilson, Peter H. "Bolstering the Prestige of the Habsburgs: The End of the Holy Roman Empire in 1806." *International History Review* 28, no. 4 (December 2006): 709–36.

———. *German Armies: War and German Politics, 1648–1806*. London: UCL Press, 1998.

———. "German Military Preparedness at the Eve of the Revolutionary Wars." In *Warfare in Europe, 1792–1815*, edited by Frederick C. Schneid. Aldershot, UK: Ashgate, 2007.

Chapter 5: Armies of the Napoleonic Wars

Atteridge, A. H. *Marshal Ney: The Bravest of the Brave*. Barnsley, UK: Pen & Sword, 2005. First published in 1913 by Brentano's.

Ben Toutouh, Hassan. "Resistance to Conscription and Local Conflicts in the Department of the Dyle (1801–1806)." *Selected Papers of the Consortium on the Revolutionary Era* (2008): 110–16.

Bertaud, Jean-Paul. "Napoleon's Officers." *Past & Present* 112 (1986): 91–111.

Blaufarb, Rafe. *The French Army, 1750–1820: Careers, Talent, Merit*. Manchester: Manchester University Press, 2002.

Blond, Georges. *La Grande Armée*. New York: Sterling Publishing, 1997.

Boerke, Arthur. "Conscription in the Habsburg Empire to 1815." In *Conscription in the Napoleonic Era: A Revolution in Military Affairs?*, edited by Donald Stoker, Frederick C. Schneid and Harold Blanton. London: Routledge, 2009.

Brown, Howard. "Politics, Professionalism, and the Fate of the Army Generals after Thermidor." *French Historical Studies* 19 (1995): 132–52.

———. *War, Revolution and the Bureaucratic State: Politics and Army Administration in France, 1791–1799*. Oxford: Oxford University Press, 1995.

Cardoza, Thomas. *Intrepid Women: Cantinières and Vivandières of the French Army*. Bloomington: Indiana University Press, 2010.

Chandler, David, ed. *Napoleon's Marshals*. New York: Macmillan, 1987.

Cook, Llewellyn. "Command in Crisis: The Army of Bohemia, May–August 1813." *Selected Papers of the Consortium on the Revolutionary Era* (2008): 215–25.

Corvisier, André. *Histoire militaire de la France.* 4 vols. Paris: Presses universitaires de France, 1992.

Coss, Edward J. *All for the King's Shilling: The British Soldier under Wellington, 1808–1814.* Norman: University of Oklahoma Press, 2010.

Creveld, Martin van. *Supplying War: Logistics from Wallenstein to Patton.* Cambridge: Cambridge University Press, 1979.

Dague, Everett Thomas. *Napoleon and the First Empire's Ministries of War and Military Administration: The Construction of a Military Bureaucracy.* Lewiston, NY: Mellen Press, 2006.

Davies, Huw J. *Wellington's Wars: The Making of a Military Genius.* New Haven, CT: Yale University Press, 2012.

Duffy, Christopher. *Eagles over the Alps: Suvarov in Italy and Switzerland, 1799.* Chicago: Emperor's Press, 1999. First printed in 1998.

Elting, John R. *Swords Around a Throne: Napoleon's Grande Armée.* New York: Free Press, 1988.

Esposito, Vincent, and John R. Elting. *Military History and Atlas of the Napoleonic Wars.* London: Greenhill Books, 1999.

Eysturlid, Lee. *The Formative Influences, Theories, and Campaigns of the Archduke Carl of Austria.* Westport, CT: Greenwood, 2000.

Forrest, Alan. *Conscripts and Deserters: The French Army and Society during the Revolution and Empire.* New York: Oxford University Press, 1989.

———. *Napoleon's Men: The Soldiers of the Revolution and Empire.* London: Hambledon and London, 2002.

Fortescue, Sir John. *A History of the British Army.* 20 vols. London: Macmillan & Co., 1899–1926.

Gallaher, John G. *Dominique Vandamme: Napoleon's Enfant Terrible.* Norman: University of Oklahoma Press, 2008.

———. *General Alexandre Dumas: Soldier of the French Revolution.* Carbondale: University of Southern Illinois Press, 1997.

———. *The Iron Marshal: A Biography of Louis N. Davout.* Carbondale: University of Southern Illinois Press, 1976.

Gates, David. *The British Light Infantry Arm, 1790–1815: Its Creation, Training, and Operational Role.* London: Batsford, 1987.

Gill, John H. *1809: Thunder on the Danube: Napoleon's Defeat of the Habsburgs*. 3 vols. London: Frontline Books, 2008–2010.

Guy, Alan, ed. *The Road to Waterloo: The British Army and the Struggle against Revolutionary and Napoleonic France, 1793–1815*. London: A. Sutton, 1990.

Hanley, Wayne. "Between Sylla and Charybdis: Marshal Ney at Lons-le-Saulnier." *Selected Papers of the Consortium on the Revolutionary Era* (2008): 272–79.

———. "Ney and Quatre Bras: An Invitation for Reevaluation." *Selected Papers of the Consortium on the Revolutionary Era* (2007): 332–43.

Hartley, Janet M. *Russia, 1762–1825: Military Power, the State, and the People*. Westport, CT: Praeger, 2008.

Hileman, Scott. "The King's Paladin: Sir Thomas Picton and the Battle of Buçacao, 1810." *Selected Papers of the Consortium on Revolutionary Europe* (2005): 191–200.

Hippler, Thomas. *Citizens, Soldiers and National Armies: Military Service in France and Germany, 1789–1830*. New York: Routledge, 2008.

Hochedlinger, Michael. *Austria's Wars of Emergence: War, State and Society in the Habsburg Monarchy, 1683–1797*. Harlow, UK: Longman, 2003.

———. "The Early Modern Cinderella." *Austrian History Yearbook* 32 (2001): 207–13.

———. "Mars Ennobled: The Ascent of the Military and the Creation of a Military Nobility in Mid-Eighteenth Century Austria." *German History* 17, no. 2 (1999): 141–76.

Horricks, Raymond. *Marshal Ney: The Real and the Romance*. New York: Hippocrene Books, 1982.

Hughes, Michael J. *Forging Napoleon's Grande Armée: Motivation, Military Culture, and Masculinity in the French Army*. New York: New York University Press, 2012.

Keep, John L. *Soldiers of the Tsar: Army and Society in Russia, 1462–1874*. Oxford: Clarendon Press, 1985.

Leggiere, Michael V. "Austrian Grand Strategy and the Invasion of France in 1814." *Selected Papers of the Consortium on the Revolutionary Era* (2007): 322–31.

———. *The Fall of Napoleon: The Allied Invasion of France 1813–1814*. Cambridge: Cambridge University Press, 2007.

———. *Napoleon and Berlin: The Franco-Prussian War in North Germany, 1813*. Norman: University of Oklahoma Press, 2002.

Lieven, Dominic. *Russia Against Napoleon: The True Story of the Campaigns of War and Peace*. New York: Viking, 2009.

Marshall-Cornwall, J. H. *Marshal Massena*. London: Oxford University Press, 1965.

Mikaberidze, Alexander. "Conscription in Russia in the Late Eighteenth and Early Nineteenth Centuries: 'For Faith, Tsar and Motherland.'" In *Conscription in the Napoleonic Era: A Revolution in Military Affairs?*, edited by Donald Stoker, Frederick C. Schneid, and Harold Blanton. London: Routledge, 2009.

———. *The Russian Officer Corps in the Revolutionary and Napoleonic Wars, 1792–1815*. London: Spellmount, 2005.

Moon, Joshua. *Wellington's Two Front War: The Peninsular Campaigns at Home and Abroad, 1808–1814*. Norman: University of Oklahoma Press, 2011.

Morgan, John. "War Feeding War? The Impact of Logistics upon the Occupation of Catalonia." *Journal of Military History* 73, no. 1 (January 2009): 83–116.

Muir, Rory. *Tactics and the Experience of Battle in the Age of Napoleon*. New Haven, CT: Yale University Press, 1998.

Oman, Carola. *Napoleon's Viceroy: Eugène de Beauharnais*. New York: Funk and Wagnalls, 1966.

Paret, Peter. *Yorck and the Era of the Prussian Reform, 1807–1815*. Princeton, NJ: Princeton University Press, 1966.

Rothenberg, Gunther E. *The Art of Warfare in the Age of Napoleon*. Bloomington: Indiana University Press, 1976.

———. *Napoleon's Great Adversary: The Archduke Charles and the Austrian Army, 1792–1814*. Bloomington: Indiana University Press, 1982.

———. "Shield of the Dynasty: Reflections on the Habsburg Army, 1649–1918." *Austrian History Yearbook* 32 (2001): 169–206.

Schneid, Frederick C. *Napoleon's Conquest of Europe: The War of the Third Coalition*. Westport, CT: Praeger, 2005.

Severn, John. *Architects of Empire: The Duke of Wellington and His Brothers*. Norman: University of Oklahoma Press, 2007.

Shanahan, William. *Prussian Military Reform, 1786–1813*. New York: Columbia University Press, 1945.

Showalter, Dennis. "Hubertusberg to Auerstädt: The Prussian Army in Decline?" *German History* 12 (1994): 308–30.

———. "The Prussian Landwehr and Its Critics." *Central European History* 4 (1971): 3–33.

———. "Reform and Stability: Prussia's Military Dialectic From Hubertusberg to Waterloo." In *The Projection and Limitations of Imperial Powers*, edited by Frederick C. Schneid. Leiden: Brill, 2012.

Stoker, Donald J., Frederick C. Schneid, and Harold Blanton, eds. *Conscription in the Napoleonic Era: A Revolution in Military Affairs?* London: Routledge, 2009.

Walter, Dierk. "Meeting the French Challenge: Conscription in Prussia, 1807–1815." In *Conscription in the Napoleonic Era: A Revolution in Military Affairs?*, edited by Donald Stoker, Frederick C. Schneid, and Harold Blanton. London: Routledge, 2009.

Weller, Jac. *Wellington in India*. London: Greenhill Books, 1993.

Wetzler, Peter. *War and Subsistence: The Sambre and Meuse Army in 1794*. New York: University Press of America, 1985.

White, Charles Edward. *The Enlightened Soldier: Scharnhorst and the Militärische Gesellschaft in Berlin, 1801–1805*. Westport, CT: Praeger, 1989.

Wirtschafter, Elise Kimerling. *From Serf to Russian Soldier*. Princeton, NJ: Princeton University Press, 1990.

Woloch, Isser. "Napoleonic Conscription: State Power and Civil Society. " *Past & Present* 111 (1986): 101–29.

———. *The New Regime: Transformations of the French Civic Order, 1789–1820s*. New York: Norton, 1994.

Chapter 6: Britain, Spain, and the Peninsular War

Alexander, Don W. *Rod of Iron: French Counterinsurgency Policy in Aragon during the Peninsular War*. Wilmington, DE: Scholarly Resources, 1985.

Barbier, Jacques. "Indies Revenues and Naval Spending: The Cost of Colonialism for the Spanish Bourbons, 1763–1805." In *Warfare in Europe, 1792–1815*, edited by Frederick C. Schneid. Aldershot, UK: Ashgate, 2007.

Black, Jeremy. "British Strategy and the Struggle with France, 1793–1815." *Journal of Strategic Studies* 31, no. 4 (August 2008): 553–69.

————. *The War of 1812 in the Age of Napoleon*. Norman: University of Oklahoma Press, 2009.

Cooper, Randolf G. *The Anglo-Maratha Campaigns and the Contest for India: The Struggle for Control of the South Asian Military Economy*. Cambridge: Cambridge University Press, 2003.

Cormack, William. *Revolution and Political Conflict in the French Navy, 1789–1794*. Cambridge: Cambridge University Press, 1995.

Crouzet, François. "Wars, Blockade, and Economic Change in Europe, 1792–1815." *Journal of Economic History* 24 (1964): 567–88.

Davies, Huw. "Wellington's First Command: The Political and Military Campaign Against Dhoondiah Vagh, February–September 1800." *Modern Asian Studies* 1 (2010): 1–33.

Dempsey, Guy. *Albuera 1811: The Bloodiest Battle of the Peninsular War*. London: Frontline Books, 2008.

Dubois, Laurent. *Avengers of the New World: The Story of the Haitian Revolution*. Cambridge, MA: Belknap Press of Harvard University Press, 2004.

Duffy, Michael. *Soldiers, Sugar, and Seapower: The British Expeditions to the West Indies and the War Against Revolutionary France*. Oxford: Oxford University Press, 1987.

Dull, Jonathan. *The Age of the Ship of the Line: The British and French Navies, 1650–1815*. Lincoln: University of Nebraska Press, 2009.

Elliott, J. H. *Empires of the Atlantic World: Britain and Spain in America, 1492–1830*. New Haven, CT: Yale University Press, 2006.

Esdaile, Charles. "De-Constructing the French Wars: Napoleon as Anti-Strategist." *Journal of Strategic Studies* 21, no. 4 (August 2008): 515–52.

————. *The Duke of Wellington and the Command of the Spanish Army*. New York: St. Martin's Press, 1990.

————. *Fighting Napoleon: Guerrillas, Bandits and Adventurers in Spain, 1808–1814*. New Haven, CT: Yale University Press, 2004.

————. *Napoleon's Wars: An International History, 1803–1815*. London: Allen Lane, 2007.

————. *The Peninsular War: A New History*. New York: Palgrave Macmillan, 2003.

————. *The Spanish Army in the Peninsular War*. Manchester: Manchester University Press, 1988.

Feldbaek, Ole. *Denmark and Armed Neutrality, 1800–1801: A Small Power Policy in a World War*. Copenhagen: Akademisk Forlag, 1980.

Fletcher, Ian. *Waters of Oblivion: The British Invasion of the Rio de la Plata*. London: Spellmount, 2006. First published in 1991 by Spellmount.

Gates, David. *The Spanish Ulcer: A History of the Peninsular War*. Philadelphia: Da Capo Press, 1986.

Hall, Christopher D. *British Strategy in the Napoleonic Wars, 1803–1815*. Manchester: Manchester University Press, 1992.

Harbron, John. *Trafalgar and the Spanish Navy: The Spanish Experience of Sea Power*. Annapolis, MD: Naval Institute Press, 1988.

Horward, Donald. *The Battle of Bussaco: Masséna vs. Wellington*. Tallahassee: University Press of Florida, 1965.

————. *Napoleon and Iberia: The Twin Sieges of Ciudad Rodrigo and Almeida, 1810*. Tallahassee: University Press of Florida, 1984.

Ingram, Edward. "The Geopolitics of the First British Expedition to Egypt - I: The Cabinet Crisis of September 1800." *Middle Eastern Studies* 30, no. 3 (July 1994): 435–60.

————. "The Geopolitics of the First British Expedition to Egypt - II: The Mediterranean Campaign, 1800–1." *Middle Eastern Studies* 30, no. 4 (October 1994): 699–723.

————. "The Geopolitics of the First British Expedition to Egypt - III: The Red Sea Campaign, 1800–1." *Middle Eastern Studies* 31, 1 (January 1995): 146–69.

————. "The Geopolitics of the First British Expedition to Egypt - IV: Occupation and Withdrawal, 1801–3." I*Middle Eastern Studies* 31, no. 2 (April 1995): 317–46.

————. "A Preview of the Great Game in Asia - I: The British Occupation of Perim and Aden in 1799." *Middle Eastern Studies* 9, no. 1 (January 1973): 3–18.

————. "A Preview of the Great Game in Asia - III: The Origins of the British Expedition to Egypt in 1801." *Middle Eastern Studies* 9, no. 3 (October 1973): 296–314.

————. "A Preview of the Great Game in Asia - IV: British Agents in the Near East in the War of the Second Coalition, 1798–1801." *Middle Eastern Studies* 10, no. 1 (January 1974): 15–35.

Jörgensen, Christer. *The Anglo-Swedish Alliance against Napoleonic France*. New York: Palgrave Macmillan, 2004.

Keegan, Jon. *The Face of Battle*. New York: Viking Press, 1976.

Knight, Roger. *The Pursuit of Victory: The Life and Achievements of Horatio Nelson*. London: Allen Lane, 2005.

Lynch, John. "British Policy and Spanish America, 1783–1808." *Journal of Latin American Studies* 1, no. 1 (1969): 1–30.

Mackesy, Piers. *British Victory in Egypt, 1801: The End of Napoleon's Conquest*. London: Routledge, 1995.

———. *The War in the Mediterranean, 1803–1810*. Westport, CT: Greenwood, 1981.

Mahan, Alfred T. *The Influence of Sea Power upon the French Revolution and Empire*. Boston: Little, Brown, 1892.

Marichal, Carlos. *Bankruptcy of Empire: Mexican Silver and the Wars between Spain, Britain, and France, 1760–1810*. New York: Cambridge University Press, 2007.

McCranie, Kevin. *Admiral Lord Keith and the Naval War against Napoleon*. Gainesville: University of Florida Press, 2006.

———. "Recruitment of Seamen for the British Navy: 1793–1815. 'Why don't you raise more men?'" In *Conscription in the Napoleonic Era: A Revolution in Military Affairs?*, edited by Donald Stoker, Frederick C. Schneid, and Harold Blanton. London: Routledge, 2009.

Moon, Joshua. *Wellington's Two-Front War: The Peninsular Campaigns at Home and Abroad, 1808–1814*. Norman: University of Oklahoma Press, 2011.

Morgan, John. "War Feeding War? The Impact of Logistics upon the Occupation of Catalonia." *Journal of Military History* 73, no. 1 (January 2009): 83–116.

Muir, Rory. *Britain and the Defeat of Napoleon, 1807–1815*. New Haven, CT: Yale University Press, 1996.

———. *Salamanca 1812*. New Haven, CT: Yale University Press, 2001.

Napier, William Francis. *History of the War in the Peninsula*. 4 vols. Philadelphia: Cary & Hart, 1828–1840.

Oman, Charles. *A History of the Peninsular War*. 7 vols. Oxford: Clarendon Press, 1902–1930.

Pelet, Jean Jacques Germain. *French Campaign in Portugal*. Translated by Donald Horward. Minneapolis: University of Minnesota Press, 1973.

Riley, Jonathon. *Napoleon as a General: From Battlefield to Grand Strategy*. Hambeldon: London, 2007.

———. *Napoleon and the World War of 1813: Lessons in Coalition Warfighting*. London: Routledge, 2000.

Rodger, N. A. M. *Command of the Ocean: A Naval History of Britain, 1649–1815*. 2 vols. New York: W. W. Norton, 2005.

———. "Recent Work in British Naval History, 1750–1815." *Historical Journal* 51, no. 3 (September 2008): 741–51.

Schneid, Frederick C. *Napoleon's Conquest of Europe: The War of the Third Coalition*. Westport, CT: Praeger, 2005.

Sherwig, John. *Guineas and Gunpowder: British Foreign Aid in the War against France, 1793–1815*. Cambridge, MA: Harvard University Press, 1969.

Syrett, David. *Admiral Lord Howe*. Annapolis, MD: Naval Institute Press, 2006.

Tone, John. *The Fatal Knot: The Guerrilla War in Navarre and the Defeat of Napoleon in Spain*. Chapel Hill: University of North Carolina Press, 1994.

Voelcker, Tim. *Admiral Saumarez versus Napoleon: The Baltic, 1807–1812*. Rochester, NY: Boydell Press, 2008.

Weller, Jac. *Wellington in India*. London: Longman, 1972.

Wright, J. F. "British Government Borrowing in Wartime, 1763–1815." *Economic History Review* 52, no. 2 (1999): 355–61.

Conclusion

Hippler, Thomas. *Citizens, Soldiers and National Armies: Military Service in France and Germany, 1789–1830*. New York: Routledge, 2008.

Schneid, Frederick C. "Conscription and the Militarization of Europe." In *Conscription in the Napoleonic Era: A Revolution in Military Affairs?*, edited by Donald Stoker, Frederick C. Schneid, and Harold Blanton. London: Routledge, 2009.

Schroeder, Paul. "Did the Vienna System Rest Upon a Balance of Power?" *American Historical Review* 97, no. 2 (June 1992): 683–706, 733–35.

Frederick C. Schneid is professor of history at High Point University in North Carolina. He received his doctorate at Purdue University where he studied military history under the direction of the eminent historian Gunther E. Rothenberg. He served as a visiting professor at Purdue until 1994, when he joined the faculty at High Point University. Since 2000 he has been a member of the Board of Directors of the Consortium on Revolutionary Europe, serving in 2004 as president. From 2005 to 2008 he was general editor of the *Selected Papers of the Consortium*. He currently serves as the southern regional director for the Society for Military History. In 2008 he became a series editor for the award-winning History of Warfare series published by Brill. He has published numerous books and articles on European military history and the Napoleonic Wars, including *Napoleon's Conquest of Europe: The War of the Third Coalition* (Praeger); *Napoleon's Italian Campaigns: 1805–1815* (Praeger); *Soldiers of Napoleon's Kingdom of Italy, 1800–1814* (HarperCollins/ Westview); and *European Warfare: 1792–1815* (Ashgate).